Also by Simon Robinson and Maria Moraes Robinson

Holonomics: Business Where People and Planet Matter

Customer
Experiences
with Soul

A New Era in Design

Simon Robinson and
Maria Moraes Robinson

Holonomics Publishing

Published in 2017 by Holonomics Publishing.

HOLONOMICS PUBLISHING

Holonomics Publishing is the UK-registered publishing division of Holonomics Education.

Office 7, 35-37 Ludgate Hill, London, EC4M 7JN
www.holonomics.pub

The right of Simon Robinson and Maria Moraes Robinson to be identified as the authors of this work have been asserted by them in accordance with the Copyright, Designs and Patents Act 1988.

ISBN: 978-0-9957-1580-6 (sc)
ISBN: 978-0-9957-1581-3 (e)

Library of Congress Control Number: 2017905363

Because of the dynamic nature of the Internet, any web addresses or links contained in this book may have changed since publication and may no longer be valid.

Front cover: Double-walled Espresso Glass, Bredemeijer®

Rev. date: 6/2/2017

This book is dedicated to the memory of
Sônia Moraes Amiden and Amim Amiden

Contents

List of Illustrations

Preface and Acknowledgements

The last three decades have seen a steady evolution in customer experience design methods and practices. These have been complemented by the introduction of systemic and visual business tools such as Balanced Scorecard and the Business Model Canvas which have radically changed the way in which entrepreneurs and corporations develop new businesses, innovate new products and services, and improve and evolve their existing business models and strategies. However, despite a growing awareness of the impact on profitability of being a customer-focused organisation, and despite the wealth of new approaches to innovation, many studies report that a substantial number of new products and services are still failing to meet customer expectations. The time therefore has now arrived for business leaders to radically reappraise what they are doing, how they are doing it, who they are doing it with, and most importantly, why.

The subtitle to *Customer Experiences with Soul* is 'A New Era in Design'. The reason is that this is a book about customer experience design which approaches the discipline in a way that has never been discussed before. Our approach is based on the philosophy of wholeness, which we introduced in our first book *Holonomics: Business Where People and Planet Matter*. After many years of working with enterprises, helping them to see their organisations as an authentic whole, and improving how they function and operate, we brought together our knowledge of strategy and change management, user experience design, product marketing and business development in *Holonomics* which was published in 2014. The book was written to help people engage in issues and problems in an entirely different manner from business as usual, resulting in evolutionary business models, powerful and effective strategies, and the development of purposeful, meaningful and sustainable brands.

One of the most important dimensions of our Holonomics approach is a concept we call 'the dynamics of seeing'. The reason is that within general business practice there is an implicit assumption that the world 'out there' is a given and that people simply have different opinions about it. One of the qualities of a truly great designer is that the manner in which they experience their reality is dynamic, always searching for new ways of seeing and understanding the world. The importance of the dynamics of seeing to developing a more profound understanding of customer experience design cannot be underestimated. All of us have the capacity to evolve if we develop an expanded level of consciousness, but we also have to develop an awareness of the barriers which can prevent us from achieving this.

A second important dimension to our Holonomics approach is our expanded interpretation of sustainability, which we define as the quality of our relationships. This is much wider than more typical definitions of sustainability, because it allows businesses to understand how they can better prepare for the volatile, uncertain, complex and ambiguous reality in which we now live. When the leaders of an organisation fully sign up to this way of understanding sustainability, they are then able to transform their businesses through the redesign and rethinking of one of the most fundamental relationships they have – that which exists between a company and its customers. Given that this relationship is fundamentally human, we wished to introduce the one vital factor which until now has been notably absent from business discourse, and that factor is soul.

Customer Experiences with Soul has been written to show how our holonomics approach can be applied to the area of customer experience design. It introduces our tool, the Holonomic Circle, which articulates the meaning of soul in a design, business and branding context. It provides a holistic framework for designers, corporate entrepreneurs, creative leaders and those starting a new business or initiative to explore the principles underlying the dynamics of soulful experiences. It does so by linking the tools, techniques and frameworks for developing customer experiences with soul with an exploration of the questions of authenticity, purpose and human values.

The Holonomic Circle is a tool which allows us to ask probing questions about the customer experience and the very 'being' of brands from a perspective which is simply not found in more traditional methodologies. To help illustrate each aspect of the holonomic circle we have included in-depth, visionary interviews from entrepreneurs, CEOs, designers, artists and philosophers. The insights from this book apply not only to the design of the customer experience itself, but also to product and service development, organisational design, branding, communications, leadership, training and strategy. It will help you to take a radically new approach to customer experience design; to fully integrate your purpose, goals and strategy with your customer experience; to implement human values across the whole organisation; and to develop long-term and more meaningful relationships with your customers.

Because of the scope and ambition of our project, there are of course a great many people we would like to thank and without whose help our book could not have been written. We are especially grateful to Dr. Paulo Chapchap, CEO of Hospital Sírio Libanês, Cris Dios, co-founder of Laces and Hair, Walter Mancini, founder and owner of Famiglia Mancini restaurants, Eduardo Srur, artist and entrepreneur, and João Bernartt, founder and CEO of Chaordic Systems, for sharing so much of their rich knowledge and wisdom with us and for taking the time to explain and explore their organisations and ways of thinking. We also thank Helen Blake, Thomas Kolster, Gunther Sonnenfeld, Andrew Markell, James Souttar, Thomas Giordano and Pedro Oliveira for their valuable contributions and insights, many of which have come from numerous conversations with us over the last two years. We offer our heartfelt thanks to the late educator Sri Sathya Sai Baba for creating such a fundamental programme in human values which has provided so much inspiration for our work.

We thank Tao Ruspoli for graciously allowing us to share material from his wonderful documentary *Being in the World* (Mangu Films, 2014), and John Timpson for allowing us to publish extracts from the BBC interview in which he discusses his philosophy of Upside Down Management. We are also very grateful to James Watt for allowing us to share the BrewDog charter, Bruce Temkin for providing us with permission to cite findings from the research of Temkin Group, Jennifer Elks for providing us with permission to republish parts of John Schulz's presentation at Sustainable Brands San Diego, Matt Watkinson for allowing us to publish his ten principles of great customer experiences, Henrik Kniberg for letting us use quotations from his video on Spotify's engineering culture, Raphael Bemporad for providing us with the permission to share insights from BBMG, Winnie Tyrrell, Photo Library Co-ordinator at Glasgow Life/Glasgow Museums for helping us obtain permission to reproduce our photograph of *The Druids – Bringing in the Mistletoe*, and to Vicky Mitchell, Business Affairs Executive, BBC Rights, Legal & Business Affairs for helping us to obtain permission to reproduce John Timpson's interview.

The front cover image of the double-walled espresso glass comes from Bredemeijer®, a company based in The Netherlands. We are most grateful to Esther de Wit, Marketing Coordinator at Bredemeijer Group for allowing us to reproduce their glass, an image which for us has many layers of meaning in relation to customer experience, service and soul. We would also like to extend a special thank you to Jonathan Robinson for his advice and great diligence in editing our manuscript, and to Justin Schofield from Lulu for his guidance in managing the publication process.

Behind the scenes many friends, colleagues and other people have provided invaluable assistance in many different ways. We thank Douglas Dias from Famiglia Mancini, Fiona Stewart, David McDowall, and Neil Taylor from BrewDog, Erika Thais Rocha from BrewDog Bar São Paulo, Cindy Barnes from Futurecurve, Christine Hickman from Timpson, and Andrea Rosen from Contagious. We would also like to thank Fritjof Capra, Bruno Cheuiche, Olavo Oliveira, Daniela Carvalho, Zoraide Stark, Dalton de Souza Amorim, Rodrigo Bicalho, Tadeu Navarro, KoAnn Vikoren Skrzyniarz, Sirikul Laukaikul, Itamar Cechetto, Lilian Lopes, Betsey Merkel, Anderson Nielson, Andrea Nalesso, Darlene Dutra, Wilmar Cidral, Philip Franses, Jan Hoglünd, Andrea Somoza-Norton, Jenny Andersson and Benjamin Butler for their valued support which in many different ways helped us to spread the message about *Holonomics* and our work around the world.

Simon Robinson and Maria Moraes Robinson
São Paulo, Brazil, May 2017

1. Customers, Experiences, Soul

What Do We Mean By Soul?

This is a book about customers, experiences and soul. These are not three easily understood discrete entities which we can simply sum together. We need to explore what we mean by these terms, and how they come together to help us move beyond designing great customer experiences, to be able to offer something deeper – *customer experiences with soul*. A little over twenty years ago an approach called 'designing the customer experience' was developed at the Human Factors department of BT Laboratories in Ipswich. In the early 1990s the focus was on human-computer interaction, a discipline mostly based in university research departments, with little connection to marketing departments, product managers, service centres and business strategists. The process 'designing the customer experience' was created to reposition Human Factors and user-centred design at the very heart of the product life-cycle within organisations, thus becoming one of the precursors to the development of design thinking, service design, customer journey mapping and concepts such as customer success.

Two decades later we felt the need to transcend what have now become well-defined approaches and definitions of customer experience, to help companies understand why their offerings are no longer resonating with people, where this deep source of a lack of authenticity, coherence and values comes from, and how to develop a profound understanding of the lived experience of every single person whose lives our organisations touch. This approach is rarely spoken about in business, but those who take on board what is being said, and who can develop the maturity and bravery to disrupt their own mental models of how things have to be, will find that they have the resources to create an entirely new way of being for their businesses, a way of being which is soulful.

In the last twenty years two significant trends have emerged which have changed the business landscape dramatically and which now require businesses and organisations to shift their attention from offering great customer experiences to customer experiences with soul. The first trend, which needs little explanation, is the explosion in our use of mobile and internet technologies which have opened up many new ways for consumers to research, connect and interact with businesses, resulting in a shift in power away from marketing campaigns and towards consumer activists, ambassadors and critics. This has led to advances in the way in which we think about and design customer journeys, developing tools such as customer journey maps which visualise in graphs and grids the many different touchpoints that customers have.

The second trend relates not to technology, but to a consumer-led paradigm shift in attitudes and beliefs not just in Generation Y and Millennials, but across all age groups as people seek to reconnect authentically to other people and to nature. Consumers are seeking out experiences rather than ever greater consumption, desiring a more dignified life where work is more meaningful, lives are happier, and relationships with businesses and brands are fully authentic, aligned with their own personal missions, values and beliefs. People today are seeking more alignment, more engagement, more connectivity, more honesty and more transparency from the companies and organisations they chose to do business with. This is now causing a crisis in companies in terms of leadership, management, sales and results as they fail to connect with their customers and clients.

Around the world there is a growing awareness of the destructive nature of current economic paradigms based on fragmentation, where powerful nations aim to dominate weaker nations rich in natural resources. The most enlightened businesses are now transforming their life-destroying business models to ones which are life-enhancing and which regenerate natural ecosystems and local economies. The concept of customer experiences with soul radically transforms our attention from a focus on interactions that individual people have with products and services, to the quality of experience of communities and the richness of the quality of their lives.

What this boils down to is a crisis of essence and a crisis of values. It is not a crisis of coherence since there are many companies operating from traditional mindsets and values which are coherent, but not authentic. Companies are confusing emotion-driven marketing campaigns which still focus on the products and services, with authentic missions which inspire people with a higher purpose beyond the core offering. This new business paradigm places a huge emphasis on business culture, as the companies which will thrive in the twenty first century will be transparent, understanding that internal equals external, meaning that every single action they carry out will constitute marketing.

In the new business paradigm you cannot design the customer experience because you *are* the customer experience, and so in order to understand the customer experience, you have to understand what it means to *be*. This is the great question of 'being'. While this may sound like a philosophical question of little relevance to leaders, as a business begins to experience early success and starts to grow, sometimes exponentially, the sense of who we are can often become lost and confused, especially as new recruits join who were not present at the inception and who do not necessarily live the mission and vision.

In order to help businesses understand this question of being, we created the holonomic circle, a tool designed to help everyone across an organisation think about the customer experience of their offerings, and all those different aspects which need to be considered in order to be able to reach that point where the customer experience has *soul*. While we are perfectly willing to describe a corporate culture as soul-destroying, when we turn this concept around and ask if a company can have soul, the question can be particularly unsettling for many, especially if we leave the concept of soul undefined. The word 'soul' has many different meanings and connotations. While it is common to hear the claim in business of "putting our heart and soul" into our work, it is quite valid to ask the question of whether or not it is possible for a customer experience to have soul, or to put it another way, if it is possible to experience soul in a transaction?

An experience has soul when one soul recognises another soul. For this reason this book reveals the hidden qualities of experience which are rarely spoken about in a business context. Emotions play an extremely significant role in decision-making; they can cloud our judgements and can lead us to decisions which later we can come to regret, allowing less scrupulous businesses to manipulate our emotions in the buying process. But when we strip away thinking and we strip away emotion we are left with *feeling*, through which when combined with an intuitive understanding of a phenomenon such as a brand, a product, or an experience of a representative of an organisation, we achieve a deeper sense of connection with the essence of that phenomenon.

The soul in *customer experiences with soul* is the essence of a business and we encounter the essence through each and every part, be it product, service, advertisement, interface or personal interaction we have with the organisation. For this reason the term 'customer experience' refers not only to the interaction our paying customers have with our products, services and brands, but also to every single interaction inside the business between colleagues, employees, suppliers, shareholders and contractors, and every interaction between those who work for a business and who are representing the business, and every person who comes into contact with the business. Every single one of us has our own personal customer experience which *(handwritten annotations at top of page):* mercury alone expressed — verbalised judgement / Venus — which ve, awareness / Mercury — logistical thinking / Mars — expression / creative wisdom in physical manifestation / Synthesised Jens + mercury — intuitive knowing

we project and for which we have to take full responsibility. For this reason, before we explore the holonomic circle in detail, we have to explore matters relating to the transition of consciousness. The reason is that if we are stuck in ego, and if we have not developed a sense of human values, no matter how worthy our purpose there is still a danger that archetypal behaviours such as being blinkered, predatory, selfish and elitist will sabotage our efforts.

More often than not, cognitive dissonance protects people with these types of behaviours. Many people are unable to believe that leaders and gurus with such worthy aims could ever act in ways which are not congruent with their stated missions and purposes in life. While this may sound a little melodramatic, it is a sad fact that many places of work are disheartening environments to be in, and this is exacerbated by managers and leaders who may be stuck in their individual egos and therefore simply unable to ascertain just how their speech, actions and non-verbal behaviours are being communicated and picked up by those around them. While technology has given us untold abilities to interact across traditional boundaries, the networks we develop are not going to be authentic and therefore sustainable without people who have an expanded level of consciousness. Discernment is required as never before in an age of personal branding, in order that we do not accidentally find ourselves being a part of a 'knotwork' – a network with ego – which can be more cliques than authentic networks of people working towards a higher purpose for the good of all.

The journey from where we are now to developing customer experiences with soul starts with ourselves and our relationships with those immediately around us. If we can understand and heal these broken and inauthentic relationships, then we can start to rediscover trust, values and what it means to genuinely share and co-create whatever we are attempting to envision, innovate and bring into this world. The philosopher Hans-Georg Gadamer (1900–2002) was concerned with developing what he called "practical philosophy" or 'praxis' which he related to "the totality of our practical life, all our human action and behaviour, the self-adaption of the human being as a whole in this world" as well as "one's politics, political advising and consulting, and our passing of laws".[1] As members of humanity sharing this planet with our fellow human beings and all other forms of life, we need to develop ethics to guide us towards living together harmoniously. The great problem is that when we are born we do not receive instructions for acting ethically in the same way in which we can be given instructions for the use of a tool. Each one of us has to reach an understanding about a given situation, which means reaching an understanding with ourselves. Reaching an understanding is not achieved by following a scientific methodology; we have to interpret our situations and we reach an understanding through conversation and dialogue.

The holonomic circle is a framework we created to lead conversations into an understanding of customer experiences with soul. At the centre is 'the trinity', which is where authenticity is described as the maximum coherence between what a person says, what they mean, and what they do. The trinity equally applies to any group, team, organisation, business, ecosystem, and can include cities, states, countries and indeed movements. Coherence is a quality which can run throughout whole organisations, both internally and externally, and across supply chains, business ecosystems the communities with which the person or entity interacts. We encounter counterfeit purposes when what the person or group says, what the person or group means and what the person or group does fail to coalesce as a unified whole.

The middle level of the holonomic circle helps us to think about those factors which underlie our tools and techniques, and to help us understand why they sometimes work and why at times they do not. This layer is not about telling you which tools and techniques to use. It is about exploring the underlying foundations behind the tools and techniques being used, and seeing which principles need to be operating in order for the tools and techniques to become more effective. What is often missing from the application of tools and techniques is an appreciation of systems as a whole. In our book *Holonomics: Business Where People and Planet Matter*, we take an approach whereby the whole is seen as coming to presence through the parts. The whole is not the sum of the parts, and neither is the whole greater than the sum of the parts. The whole is not a thing which acts as some kind of super-part, and neither can it be imposed on the parts. An authentic whole can only be encountered through the way in which it expresses itself through each part. If there is no conceptualisation of the whole system, and only a view on results with businesses having conflicting targets across competing departments, an organisation as a whole loses energy, it is not sustainable in the long term and will never manage to achieve coherent and soulful customer experiences.

Gadamer described his philosophy as the art of reaching an understanding – either of some thing or with someone. This reaching of an understanding is always an interpretation, which happens in conversation, in dialogue. It is for this reason that the outer circle of the holonomic circle contains the transcendentals, a guiding set of interwoven ideas which we can use to explore and talk about our products and services, our customer experience. Understanding the truth of experience requires curiosity, questioning and an ability to interweave the transcendentals into each other. If we really are to understand customer experiences, and understand how customers are interpreting our products, services and brands, we need to explore the way in which language and reality *belong together;* how we participate in reality and interpret the world. The 'truth' is something we can never definitively arrive at, due to the limitations of language. But through authentic dialogue, humility and an expanded level of consciousness we can remain open to an ever-changing vista of viewpoints and interpretations where beauty, truth and goodness all belong together within our experience.

Why Customer Experience Matters

Fábio Porchat is one of Brazil's most prolific, omnipresent and hardest-working comedians. After rising to fame on Brazilian television he wanted to take comedy to the next level, but realised that the medium of traditional media and television channels would be too restrictive. In 2012, along with a small group of friends, Porchat decided to create the on-line comedy channel Porta dos Fundos ('Backdoor'), allowing them far greater artistic freedom. With over 12.5 million subscribers, in 2015 Porta dos Fundos celebrated their two billionth view on Youtube, making them the largest channel in Brazil, and the fifth largest comedy channel in the world. Some sketches now also have English subtitles, allowing Porta dos Fundos to reach a new audience worldwide.

Porchat really came to prominence in the sketch *Estaremos Fazendo o Cancelamento* (We're Doing the Cancellation)[2] in which 'Fábio' – covered in blue paint as a satirical swipe at the company TIM – attempts to call an unnamed mobile phone company to cancel his mobile phone contract. Like many of us in this situation, he enters into despair as he suffers from what many us experience in every country – terrible customer service. Fábio keeps trying to connect, and each time he gets put through to an operator called Judith. After a few times trying to actually speak to Judith (who keeps putting the phone down on him) he explains that all he wants to do is cancel his current phone contract and that no, he does not want to upgrade to a new service plan. After a few more attempts to get through he then has to go through the whole rigmarole of telling her his birthday. We empathise with Fábio and laugh with him as he becomes ever more angry when he is asked for the same information which he has provided many times already. His angst increases as the line drops and he has to call again, and then he is put on hold. His angst turns to exasperation as he is then asked to send a fax:

No, I'm not going to send you a fax. No one has fax any more. Faxes don't exist any more!

And as he approaches boiling point and gets put through to Judith one more time his language gets a lot more flowery, so to speak. With his pleas to cancel his contract going unheeded, he caves in and asks to be put on to just a basic plan, Judith having won this war of attrition. However, there is then the infamous Brazilian bureaucracy to contend with, as Fábio is asked for various official documents before he can continue. A bit more flowery language then ensues as Judith threatens to transfer Fábio, resulting in yet again another failed quest to cancel his contract. So Fábio calls one more time:

Hi, good evening. What's your name? Judith?......

Without doubt most of us have experienced frustrating situations like this at least a few times in our lives. It is a terrible customer experience, an agonising experience, and yet many companies with customer service centres never manage to transcend this level of treatment of the customer. We often show this sketch to our MBA students when teaching customer experience design, service design and business strategy, and ask them the question "what exactly is causing Judith to act in this manner?" Have a think about this yourself for a few moments. Perhaps Judith is having personal problems and wants to take it out on her customers; perhaps she has a terrible manager; perhaps she has been given demanding sales incentives and has been told to follow a script without deviating; or perhaps she has been given targets based on call length – the list of possible explanations is endless.

In the UK in 2013, people complained about products and services approximately once every second, representing around 38 million complaints in total. That's a lot of complaining. Ombudsman

Services who carried out this research then found that in 2014 the number of complaints made about products and services almost doubled to reach 66 million. Their research showed a marked shift in the willingness of consumers to take action when they have a grievance. Almost half (47%) of Britons with a complaint took action by either going to the supplier or a third party, which compares to just over a third (34%) in 2013.[3]

This research found two main reasons for this increase. The first was that with an ever-growing use of internet-based services the removal of human involvement appears to be increasing the probability of minor errors and mistakes which need to be corrected. The second factor was the greater opportunity that customers now had to complain with the growing use of social media. More than 20 million complaints were made last year through social media channels like Facebook, Twitter and consumer forums. What should be even more worrying for companies is that despite the fact that people are complaining more, there is still a silent majority of people who do not think that complaining is worth the hassle. Ombudsman Services discovered an additional 71 million problems that were never acted upon, with customers choosing to suffer in silence.[4]

Matt Watkinson defines the customer experience as being "the qualitative aspect of any interaction that an individual has with a business, its products or services, at any point in time".[5] Within this definition the term 'individual' is carefully chosen to highlight the fact that customer experiences are phenomena experienced not just by those people who are making purchases. Watkinson makes the point that there are many interactions that are commonly neglected but which offer great opportunities to stand out from the competition.

Deborah Eastman, chief customer officer of Satmetrix highlights five key findings which provide the business case for focusing on customer experience:[6]

- 91% of marketing leaders believe that in two years they will be competing primarily on the basis of the customer experience.
- A 2% increase in customer retention has the same effect as decreasing costs by 10%.
- Acquiring new customers can cost as much as 5 times more than satisfying and retaining current customers.
- 44% of consumers say that the majority of customer experiences are bland.
- 69% of consumers say that emotions count for over half of their experiences.

The impact of emotion on loyalty is huge. When customers feel great about a company, they are more like to purchase more from a company, recommend the company, trust the company, forgive the company after a mistake and try new products and services.[7] Each year Temkin Group publish their *Temkin Experience Ratings*, a cross-industry, open standard benchmark of customer experience which is based on three dimensions of experience:

Success: the ability of the customer to carry out their desired task.
Effort: how easy it is to interact with a company.
Emotion: how people feel about their interactions.

Their research consisted in asking 10,000 US consumers to rate their recent interactions with companies across twenty industries and evaluate their experiences across the three dimensions. When looking at the research at the level of industry sectors, supermarket chains took six of the top eleven spots (achieving "good" ratings), while internet service providers, TV service providers and health plan providers all received "very poor" ratings overall. Interestingly, no industry managed to score "excellent" on average. The 2016 research is notable in showing that for the first time there were falls in rating across all three dimensions (success, effort and emotion).[8] Based on this research, Bruce Temkin believes that long-term success requires companies to build and sustain four customer experience competencies:

Purposeful Leadership: Leaders operate consistently with a clear set of values.

Employee Engagement: Employees are aligned with the goals of the organisation.

Compelling Brand Values: Brand promises drive how the organisation treats customers.

Customer Connectedness: Customer insights are infused across the organisation.

These are all essential components when approaching the design of a customer experience, but beyond these competencies lies an elusive, more profound and intuitive ingredient, something much harder to define, but which leads to the creation of more fun, surprising and meaningful experiences. That ingredient is soul.

Customers can only sense soul in the experience when every single person in the organisation is fully engaged. The 2016 Temkin Employee Engagement Index analysed the engagement levels of more than 5,000 U.S. employees.[9] Their results showed that employee engagement levels vary by organisation, industry and individual, and that companies with stronger financial performances and better customer experience have employees who are considerably more engaged than their peers:

   77% of employees in companies that have significantly better financial performance than their peers are highly or moderately engaged, compared with only

49% of employees in companies with lagging financial performance.

- Customer experience leaders have 1.5 times as many engaged employees as do customer experience laggards.
- Compared with disengaged employees, highly engaged employees are more than four times as likely to recommend the company's products and services and do something good for the company that is not expected of them, 2.5 times as likely to stay at work late if something needs to be done after the normal workday ends, and seven times as likely to recommend that a friend or relative apply for a job at their company.
- 63% of highly engaged employees always try their hardest at work, compared with 42% of disengaged employees.
- Companies with 500 to 1,000 employees have the most engaged employees, while those with more than 10,000 employees have the least.
- 25 to 34-year-old employees are the most engaged group, while 45 to 54-year-old employees are the least engaged.
- Senior executives are 1.6 times more likely than individual contributors to be highly or moderately engaged.
- Of the 15 industries measured in the study, construction has the highest level of moderately and highly engaged employees (71%).

One extremely effective way to engage people, no matter which role or level in the organisation they may occupy is to use gamification and storytelling to create experiential learning experiences. These techniques can also help organisations who may be stuck in traditional, linear mindsets to transform and become more dynamic, authentic, and agile. For example, an organisation may wish to receive help developing a sustainable and long-term business strategy. It may then wish to communicate this strategy across the entire organisation, to people working at all levels. Communication elements such as brochures and video presentations which may be suitable for senior executives are probably not going to be suitable for collaborators working at the lower operational levels. In this example, the communication of the strategy can be converted into powerful gaming experiences which recognise and honour the importance of each collaborator, stakeholder, client and customer. This is a holonomic way of comprehending the organisation; a way of seeing it not as a command-and-control top-down hierarchy, but which sees the essence of the brand, the mission, vision and values as 'coming-to-presence' (being expressed) through each and every member.

Jesse N. Schell is an American video games designer who has had an illustrious career, working at Walt Disney Imagineering for seven years in the capacity of programmer, manager, designer and Creative Director on several projects. Following his time at Disney, he was invited to join Carnegie Mellon University's new Entertainment Technology Center where he developed a range of design methodologies. Anyone interested in the design of customer experiences will really benefit from studying the way in which developers design games, since the thinking that goes into the creation of games – be they computer games, live action games or theme park attractions – is applicable across the creation of any experience which anyone (a client, customer, employee, stakeholder, audience) may have. Schell is now focusing on the development of what he calls transformational games; games which are illuminating as well as entertaining, having the power to transform education and the classroom. He uses the concept of lenses to offer us one hundred different perspectives on games design.[10] These emphasise the necessity for diversity in perception rather than the need for consensus views when solving problems and when designing not just games but any project. The foundation of his philosophy and methodology is the first lens, the 'Lens of Essential Experience', which calls on the games designer to stop thinking about the game, and to think about the player, by asking these three questions:[11]

- ↓ What experience do I want the players to have?
- ↓ What is essential to that experience?
- ↓ How can my game capture that essence?

There is the essence of your customer experience and the essence of your brand. The essence of the brand only exists in the experience of your customers, whoever they may be, and this is as true of a bottle of beer as it is for a meal at a restaurant, a journey by plane, a wait at a dentist, the installation of optical fibre, a trip to the theatre, the signing of a book by a favourite author – indeed any experience we wish to imagine.

In times of economic crisis in contracting economies it can be the customer experience and the way in which customers are attended to which provides the key differentiator between losing clients and growing a business. One example is Laces and Hair, a São Paulo chain of hair spas which specialise in the care of hair, 90% of their treatments being exclusive, with natural and organic products. When the economic crisis in Brazil started to take hold, in 2014 their management team saw that they would need to become more professional, leading them to make a number of structural changes. They noticed that clients were coming a little less frequently, but instead of simply cutting staff and reducing wages they invested in training, new technology and exclusive treatments. The result in Q1 of 2015 was a 24% increase in revenue.[12]

Soul in the Expression of Service, Design and Beauty

The founder of Laces and Hair is cosmetologist Cris Dios, who has also developed her own range of natural hair care products. We had the opportunity to speak to Cris on a number of occasions, as well as the leadership team and many of the professionals who work there, and Cris explained to us exactly why, in her words, "people perceive that we have a special soul".

The customer experience of Laces and Hair is whole, which we will describe in detail – it is the soul of the company fully and authentically expressing itself through every part. Their philosophy is lived fully not just by Cris, but also by her family, the company's investors, suppliers and manufacturing partners, and of course every member of the team in each hair spa. The word for 'laces' in Portuguese is also found in the Portuguese phrase *laços de família* which translates as 'family ties' in English. And so the philosophy is also expressed in the name of the hair spa itself:

> We included the word 'lace' because of the sense that it embraces; this includes all your relationships with people, collaborators, families. What is a strand of hair? It is a hair which weaves into other hairs and creates poetry. My mother created the name as it invokes the image of family ties. Our name is related to people, humans, our relationships with clients, our relationships with our staff, with our products and with our environment. Everything is interrelated.

Laces and Hair have four different units in São Paulo, designed to be "an oasis in the hustle and bustle of the metropolis". Each one is adorned with natural vegetation. They are constructed with natural wood and brick, and clients are welcomed with a table of organic dishes, fruits and cakes. Each salon uses the latest sustainable technologies such as water recycling, solar energy and natural sunlight for lighting so that clients are able to relax and feel as if they are at home, rather than a more artificial salon environment.

The story of Laces and Hair started with Cris's grandfather who came to Brazil from Spain in the 1920s. He was a greatly sought-after barber who was visionary for his time, developing his to care for . . .

slow food movement.

own natural shampoos and creams. These were designed to help cure medical issues related to people's hair and scalps, something which the medical profession at the time was not able to offer. After learning how to make these natural shampoos, conditioners and hair masks from him, Cris's mother developed this philosophy of caring for the hair and not just focusing on "artificial styling", resulting in the first Laces and Hair salon opening in 1987.

 So right from the start the hair spa had the same desire of her grandfather, to care for hair, and in fact "to take care of the person and not just the styling". Cris notes that stylists normally style for immediate effect, for example, a wedding or a party. But Laces and Hair look at the person sitting in the chair in a more holistic way. Cris has always grown up with this view of the primary importance of the health of the hair, but when she went out to study beauty sa- lons, she realised that "beauty is more of a process than something immediate". She also realised that her family's approach was more complete:

> Hair is simply an expression of life and nutrition, of what the person does in life, their daily habits, how they accept themselves as a person, and so we have this worry of looking at restoring the hair to health. Rather than trying to change the hairstyle, our focus is on bringing back the vitality of the hair. We need to look at hair as an expression of what is on the inside of someone rather than just as an external aspect. So we always start by analysing the habits of our clients, what products they currently use, how they treat their hair, and how much importance they give to their hair. More often than not, a problem with the hair is due to the habits of the person rather than a physical issue directly related to the hair itself.

The hair care philosophy of the hair spa is based on the idea of 'slow beauty' which follows in the footsteps of the slow food movement.

The focus is not on creating a momentary hairstyle for when the client steps out of a beauty salon, but in teaching clients how to care for their hair at home.

> We teach clients how they can deal with their hair. We use diagnostic questionnaires to understand why the hair is not making them happy. It's really easy for a professional to start from zero and stream-roller the hair. But no, each hair has a story and value. It has soul, it was born in a certain place. So it is important that we take all of this into account. We teach our clients how to wash their hair more carefully, how to brush the hair without damaging it and how to use natural products which do not pollute the environment. Nowadays women and men arrive home stressed and if they use a shampoo with essential oils it can improve their well-being. Clients have to brush their hair with consciousness and with care. They have to be present in the moment they are taking care of the hair.

Laces and Hair were the first hair spa in Brazil to introduce natural hair colouring products in 2016, following a five-year search for more sustainable and healthy solutions. As well as nourishing hair fibres without fading them, they are also an excellent solution for people who suffer allergic reactions to products containing chemicals:

> I always had the great desire to be able to apply natural hair dyes, and now I am realising this dream, which is the essence of Laces and Hair. Through our products our clients can take home with them a little of the experience they have in the salon.

The ingredients of natural hair dyes were originally discovered in India, while the technical solutions were developed by the French cosmetic industry. Following her years of study and research, Cris was able to evolve the products further and to create the new line *Coloração Vegetal LCS*. Natural hair dyes not only colour but also nourish the hair, and are important for the preservation and regeneration of damaged hair. Their properties do not change the structure of hair – they preserve the melanin; they respect the keratin of the hair which helps in the strengthening; they have a balanced pH; they do not fade with exposure to sun and washing, and they can be used by pregnant women, nursing mothers and people unable to use products with chemicals.

It takes forty-eight hours for natural hair dyes to have an effect. The client can leave the salon with beautiful looking hair, but since the products do not utilise peroxide, it is the oxygen in the air which performs the task of oxidation and fully colouring the hair. So clients are taught to respect the natural rhythms of nature and to fully embrace the philosophy of slow beauty. For Cris, it is the inner beauty which reflects and impacts on our outer beauty, and for this reason the hair spas run regular meditation sessions with Marcia De Luca, a practitioner of yoga, mediation and Ayurveda with over thirty years of experience. As Cris said, "Meditation is resetting the mind and starting a sincere dialogue with the soul".

Helping a client to relax in a beauty salon is no simple task, and there is no magic formula which can be applied to make clients stay in the hair spa rather than rushing off after a treatment. Beauty salons can be noisy and busy places, but at Laces and Hair "the ability to put your legs up and relax is part of the treatment". While the hair spa was founded on a philosophy of care for their clients' hair, their search for developing a natural environment began in 2011, starting with an empathy approach to the buildings in which the salons were based:

> We have four hair spas, but each one retains the characteristic and personality of the individual neighbourhood where

beach house or farmhouse

they are located. One of the hair spas is a house which is more than sixty years old for example. So we look at the original vision of the architecture of the house and try and work with this identity and preserve it. This is an analogy for how we treat a client's hair. We do not want to transform it totally, so let's see what good aspects it has already.

The design team always look for vintage furniture, while keeping a modern touch in each unit. It took five years of experimenting, but the desire was always the same – to create the environment of a beach house or a farm house, "somewhere cosy and relaxing where people can sit down and not want to leave".

From the start, each unit was designed as a home rather than a salon, with the desire that people entering should receive a "welcoming embrace". Each spa has its own personality, with individual antique chairs, avoiding long banks of identical basins:

> The clients can choose where they wish to sit, as opposed to each stylist having their own station. It's like in our home, we sit in the armchair where we feel good. So the idea is that the client can sit where they wish and therefore feel great. With no fixed place, clients can decide which corner has great energy, and people come to them to take care of them. It started like this and afterwards we expanded the idea to the environment, installing lots of plants and individual spaces, with chairs being different from each other. Mirrors, for example, have wooden frames made from old doors. It would be much easier and cheaper if we asked our suppliers to produce everything exactly the same. It's just that it would not have soul. Every piece of furniture has a story and has a soul. When clients are seated the perception may be subliminal, but they can see that these objects are singular and have a story behind them.

beauty is equilibrium.

In talking to Cris it soon becomes clear that they have built their business with a deeply authentic desire for the well-being of clients. When people are on their path, they experiment and are motivated by giving the best to the service, searching for what they should do – for example, taking five years to define a good environment. The motivation of Laces and Hair is simply on what is good for the client and not in terms of what will yield short-term financial results. Closely coupled with the design of the environment are the ambience of the hair spa and the behaviour and conduct of staff:

> The music in our spas is tranquil and people speak softly, unlike beauty salons, which can often be restless and noisy. Of course hairdryers make a noise, but this is not the whole time. The environments are more calm. This is in our DNA. Professionals go to the training centre to learn about the posture of Laces and Hair. Teaching a technique is easy, because it is a mechanical act of repetition. The more a person repeats it, the more ability they have. The most difficult thing is to teach people about how they should conduct themselves. The person must understand and identify themselves with this conduct, and perceive that in an environment where people wish to relax, talking loudly and having parallel conversations will unsettle or disturb the client. The client is the star of the play, and everything happens because of them. It is not myself, not our managers, it is the client who seeks our work, they are the raison d'être for everything else that exists.

Cris's philosophy of beauty starts with the development of inner self-confidence, inner peace and inner health. We asked Cris how she defines and thinks about beauty:

> Beauty, I think, is equilibrium, the balance between what we believe and who we are internally, and what we show in

our external expressions and what we do as an individual. It's not enough to be this marvellous woman with wonderful hair and beautiful skin if we don't worry about our legacy for the planet and what we are leaving behind – it's a whole. In our journey and process towards self-knowledge we improve ourselves and we come to accept ourselves as a human being. This makes us more beautiful. Beauty is the equilibrium between who we are internally and what we could improve, and this expresses itself in our external beauty. It's the equilibrium between our external physical form which we have externally and our essence. Maturity starts to show this to us when we start to have lines on our faces and whiter hair; we are not the same as when we were eighteen years old. We have other types of beauty. Knowing how to deal with this internal beauty is fundamental. This is real beauty.

For Cris, inner beauty cannot be separated from well-being. We finished our interview by asking Cris if she could articulate the soul and essence of Laces and Hair:

Through the beauty of hair, the health of hair, when a person enters our spa we hope that we are able to offer people the opportunity to become better people; to know themselves better, value themselves and respect other people. In essence, what we offer our clients is the opportunity to go deeper into themselves, and realise that they do have something good and that it is not necessary to be different, such as having hair like a glamorous soap opera actress or a body like an young Instagram fashion blogger. We have many beautiful things inside ourselves, and so Laces and Hair is an opportunity to have an experience of well-being and an experience of soul. This is soul – soul is what we have inside ourselves, but we never learn anywhere how to access it. We are born, and then we forget everything we came to do; we discover how to be a human being during the events and occurrences in our lives, that which we came in this world to do. When a person enters our door, they have an experience of care and that someone does approach them with great care for them. It helps you to accept who you are in reality.

One of the greatest challenges for any company wishing to grow is the continued nurturing of its soul, the very reason for its early success. In chapter four therefore we look at how BrewDog recognised this very issue and sought to capture more formally the essence of their being in their *Be More BrewDog* charter. Soul is an elusive concept to capture, quantify and describe, but when it exists, we can sense, feel and intuit its presence. It has to be authentic, and it is not a quality which is added on to an existing experience as an additional component. The more values we have in our approach to our work and our businesses, and the greater human connection that we have with our customers – whether it is direct contact with people in a hair spa, more distant contact by telephone in a service centre, or indirectly via an intermediary website – the more soul there will be in the customer experience.

Those companies which are fully authentic are ones in which there is no separation between the customer experience and the company itself. Which companies are truly fully authentic? The ones who are bloody-minded. The ones with an unwavering rock solid belief in their missions and visions. You do not add on purpose to a pre-existing product; you live your purpose with passion, and this is what customers connect with.

Authenticity is the most powerfully disruptive force in business today, but it is only fully grasped intuitively with an expanded level of consciousness. Today's crisis in business is a crisis of authenticity, and so the following chapters explain what is blocking the ability to understand, perceive and act authentically, and then how the whole organisation can come together to evolve an entirely new way of *being* in the world. Only then can a company truly say that they offer customer experiences with soul.

2. Authentic Purpose

Keeping It Real

In 2015, Havas Media Group published research which showed that brands which enhance the wellbeing of people, communities and societies have a "Share of Wallet" which is on average 46% higher compared to those brands which are not perceived as meaningful to the lives of people.[13] Customers are now responding to those companies who are genuinely transparent in all that they do. It is not enough to talk about your company's purpose and mission. Everyone in the organisation has to live it. Absolutely everything communicates something about your business and ultimately your brand, which in turn affects people's perception of it.

People want something to believe in, something they can relate to and the opportunity to be a part of a change, a crusade, a revolution. While knowing about and having confidence in the technical features of products still remains important, they want to hear about your mission. In their study of 22,000 respondents across 22 international markets, BBMG and GlobeScan found that 39% of the adult population could be classified as 'aspirationals', a cross-generational group who have a desire to make a positive impact on the lives of others and to connect with an ideal or community which is bigger than themselves.[14] 26% of people are highly-committed 'advocates', the traditional focus for sustainable consumerism, 25% are price and performance-minded 'practicals' who see sustainability as a bonus and are less likely to take the time to search for sustainable products, with the remaining 10% being less engaged 'indifferents', placing a much lower priority on products with social or environmental benefits.

The research on 'aspirationals' demonstrates a fundamental shift in culture and the values, needs and priorities of people towards authenticity, wellbeing, sustainability and social purpose. While this shift is more marked in the new generation of adults, it is also rising in older generations as well. Leading a crusade creates a context of a higher purpose and meaning, and it places a business firmly within it. It also helps to create, establish and promote a category, which can be more powerful, purposeful and compelling than simply pushing sales of a product. In recent years businesses have taken to storytelling as a technique to engage their customers. When done well, storytelling can certainly be an extremely powerful force for good. Storytelling is about authenticity and engaging people with what you are doing; it is not about pure fiction. Two Brazilian companies, however, managed to raise the ire of their loyal customers by developing fictitious stories – one inventing a fake history, the second inventing stories as to where their products and supplies came from.

The first case is that of ice cream company Diletto, who on their packaging told the story of how their recipes were first invented in 1922 in Italy by Vittorio Scabin, a grandfather of Leandro Scabin, one of the founders. A photograph from 1922 of the van that Vittorio Scabin used to sell ice-cream was added to Diletto's website. The truth of the situation was that Diletto was created in 2008, and while one of Leandro Scabin's grandfathers was an Italian with the surname of Scabin, he was a gardener who knew nothing about ice cream. The photograph was a fake.

In order to rectify this situation with disgruntled customers, the company posted a letter on its website (now removed) in which the founders argued that the character 'Vittorio Scabin' was created in order to reinforce in a very clear manner the values of the company and that it had "in no way negated their DNA". While fictional, the company claimed that the history of the brand was inspired by "real values" meaning that the actual grandfather lived in a region of Italy famous for the way in which snow from the Alps was used in the manufacture of gourmet ice-creams.[15]

The second example of fictional storytelling is somewhat more serious. Do Bem are a relatively new company, having launched their first coconut water drink in 2009. When we first saw their packaging, it seemed to us that they had really studied Innocent from the UK in terms of the 'wackaging' – bright and brash packaging using chatty, casual, 'matey' language that describes itself in the first person. As they say on their website, Do Bem want to do good, which is reflected in their name – *Do Bem* – which can be translated as 'Of Goodness' or 'Wellness'. As well as producing natural drinks which are healthy, their website states that they wish to develop closer relationships with their customers. So what was the problem with their storytelling?

The problem was that Do Bem had a story about where their oranges came from. Their packaging for their orange juice spoke of how their oranges came from the farm of Mr. Francisco, which could be found in the state of São Paulo. This justified the premium pricing of the product, as Do Bem were claiming to be supporting small organic farmers. The reality was that the oranges were produced on an industrial scale, and came from wholesalers such as Brasil Citrus, who also supply the majority of the biggest supermarkets. It is important to point out that no one is questioning the quality of produce of Brasil Citrus. What Do Bem discovered to their cost was that there are limits to storytelling and there are limits to what consumers will put up with, especially engaged consumers looking to make more conscious purchasing decisions. Do Bem replied publicly to this scandal by stating that now that they have grown, they did utilise a wide range of suppliers, but in fact Mr. Francisco did actually exist, and that with their packaging they were highlighting suppliers who were "special in their history".[16]

So what can we learn from all of this? Sustainability is not a gap in the market to be exploited commercially. If we act from a place of integrity and authenticity, then there should be no need to resort to fictitious stories about the origins of our products, services, projects and activities. If there is a lack of authenticity, then this will soon be found out by those we are seeking to hoodwink. Brands that treat their customers like idiots are not sustainable brands. If your brand is predicated on treating those you seek to serve with distain, any brand value you build up will not be sustainable. In our networked age, people are coming together to demand a new level of transparency and ethics in public and commercial spheres. Brands are reacting to this, with responsible brands not only talking about being ethical, but who actually are ethical, and who are practising what they preach. James Watt, co-founder of the Scottish brewery BrewDog describes the way in which his company is building its brand by living the brand:

> Your brand is the collated gut instinct of the world at large towards your company and everything you do. This means that you, and everyone in your business, need to live your brand. You have to live the values and the mission, internally and externally, and then let the customer decide what your brand is about. Only by being consistent, engaging, open, honest and congruent can you start to build a brand in the twenty-first century.
>
> Anything that you do, anywhere in your business, which is not completely aligned with your mission and your values is like a tiny suicide. It is not death by a million tiny cuts any more; death can come from as few as ten inconsistencies or indiscretions. Little things can damage you exponentially. Mistakes are magnified and stabbed back into your heart. Don't let tiny brand suicides stab your business soul.[17]

It is possible to interpret Watt as making a mistake between the definition of a brand and the definition of reputation. What we see in this quotation is an extremely intuitive approach to branding with a sensitivity towards those elements relating to emotion and feeling. Watt understands the brand as a phenomenon which is experienced, and in this sense he is not separating brand from reputation intellectually. He is alert to the extremely fine line BrewDog must tread between irreverent and irresponsible, and at times some of their marketing campaigns have been seen by people as having overstepped the mark, in poor taste and lacking in wisdom.

On social networks many lovers of craft beer express their dislike of BrewDog's 'punk' attitude but it can be quite interesting to see the conversations on BrewDog's internet forums which are often far from what we normally think of as punk attitudes. For example, shortly before the competition began Watt asked people if they thought that BrewDog should install televisions for the Euro 2016 football championship. The resounding response was "No". BrewDog bars are places to appreciate fine beers and not ones where people simply drink a large number of pints and act in a rowdy manner.

Brands need time and space to mature, as do the people running the businesses. Mistakes will certainly be made, and BrewDog have made many by their own admission. It is the response and an ability to learn from mistakes which have always made the difference and will always continue to do so. In BrewDog we find an extremely successful brand in which there is a very high degree of coherence between what they say, what they mean and what they do. In chapter five we will be examining human values which include non-violence and righteousness. Non-violence can refer to acts of violence within advertising images, and this is where BrewDog can still develop themselves further, elevating themselves to ever greater expressions of who they are, using humour in an irreverent manner but which avoids the need to shock.

The Trinity of Authentic Purpose

You know that you have encountered a counterfeit purpose when there is a perceptible difference between what a person says, what they actually mean, and what they actually do – i.e. how they act with each and every person they interact with (Figure 1). You know that you have encountered an authentic purpose when what someone says, means and does all line up; when you cannot detect any difference at all between them. There can be huge implications for brands if the celebrities who endorse their products fail to live the same brand values as the companies and products they are representing.

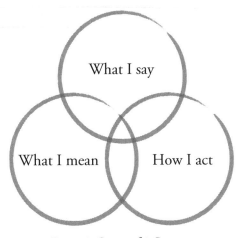

Figure 1: Counterfeit Purpose

An advertisement broadcast in 2014 in Brazil for Friboi meat featured the megastar singer Roberto Carlos, a vegetarian for decades. Roberto Carlos, playing himself, is in a restaurant with three other friends, and on being questioned by a confused waiter he explains that he has returned to eating meat because the meat is Friboi. It was widely reported that Roberto Carlos continued to be vegetarian, despite what he declared in the advertisement, causing ire in Brazil, with many Brazilians expressing their anger on social networks. If

internal

integrity

external

brands are to promote sustainable behaviours in consumers, they have to have integrity in all that they do, and their words must match their actions.

Customer expectations are changing rapidly. Technology is driving different behaviours, and with everyone now having access 24/7 each interaction that a business has with their customers provides an opportunity to influence those customers' opinions and decisions. The result is now a world where the distinction between internal and external is no longer valid. As James Watt says:

> People are looking for more alignment, more engagement, more connectivity, more honesty and more transparency. 'Internal equals External' is our radically disruptive manifesto for a 21ˢᵗ century business. The blurring of the internal external distinction has been the key thing which has underpinned this journey for us. Company culture is what happens when the company thinks that no one is looking. The problem is that today someone is always looking.[18]

Authenticity is our number one key collaboration factor we look for when developing long-term partnerships. At Holonomics Education we are fanatical about authenticity; it underscores everything we do. It is not enough to talk the talk, nor walk the walk, you absolutely have to live your purpose in each and every waking moment. For this reason the trinity of saying, doing and meaning lies at the heart of the holonomic circle (Figure 2).

Figure 2: The Holonomic Circle – The Trinity

The trinity of authentic purpose may seem quite straightforward on the surface, but there are some extremely interesting and complex dynamics and questions that arise from it. James Souttar is a brand strategist and design consultant based in the UK, and in a conversation with us he wanted to focus on the dangers of conformism which might arise:

> I spent twenty years standing up in front of audiences talking about brands, and I came to realise that what we were talking about was unsustainable – nobody could do it, and it was just like a big stick that organisations were beating themselves with. "Mea culpa! Mea culpa! Why can't we live our brand? What's wrong with us? Maybe we need a new restructuring...."

> Life gets much easier when we allow that human beings are contradictory, that life changes, and that these are good things. We feel one thing today, another tomorrow. So why try and bludgeon it all into 'consistency'? If we want to be 'authentic' we need to look at how we actually are, and what we do, and wrap our words around that.

When you work with a detailed process or methodology, the danger is that the brand values become codified. What this means is that the values become something objectified which we experience as being somehow outside ourselves. This is when we try to engineer the values in the construction of the brand, focusing on elements such as the visual look and feel, rather than using dialogue to continually explore them from different angles in order to help every person in the organisation understand their deeper meaning. James' comments alert us to the potential for contradictory and paradoxical situations arising if our values are not coherent. The following questions below can act as guidelines for dialogues within your organisation as the starting point to find out where the contradictions may be arising in your own brand:

- Is it ever truly possible to coalesce saying, doing and meaning and end up having no contradictions between them?
- To what extent can contradictions catalyse creativity, innovation and momentum, without being counterfeit?
- Which contradictions should we celebrate rather than seeking to smother out?
- To what extent do we as leaders have the ability to be brutally honestly with ourselves when reflecting on the differences between what we say, do and mean?
- To what extent are we able to really ensure that what we say is actually what we mean, given the inherent ambiguity of language and the challenges of ambiguous communication?
- How good are our listening skills when receiving feedback from our customers, clients, stakeholders and the wider community? Are we really able to determine how they have understood what we have said, or do

we construct our own conclusions based on our beliefs, values and culture?

- To what extent do our goals, objectives and targets contradict one another, and if they do, to what extent can they still authentically contribute to our overall purpose?
- To what extent do we as leaders allow our teams to have creative freedom, while not losing sight of our long-term mission, vision and purpose?

We encounter brands not just through our rational minds, but by connecting through feeling, interacting through sensing, and comprehending the authenticity of a brand in our intuition. This authenticity can only come through a deep belief in human values. The meaning of a brand cannot be imposed on others and is not static. Brands have to be allowed to live. To paraphrase Dee Hock, brands are eternal, a perpetual becoming, or they are nothing. Brands are not a thing to be known or controlled. They are a magnificent, mysterious odyssey to be experienced.[19]

Why brands at all
+ not just humans
on a smaller scale.

Well I suppose there is no
reference to brand scale being
global and stress on family
business.

3. The Transition of Consciousness

The human being knows himself only insofar as he knows
the world; he perceives the world only in himself, and himself only in the world. Every new object, well contemplated
and clearly seen, opens up a new organ within us.[20]

Johan Wolfgang von Goethe

The Journey to Authentic Dialogue

Goethe wrote these words above in 1823 in his paper *Significant
Help Given by an Ingenious Turn of Phrase* in which he recalled that
since reaching the age of maturity he had always paid attention to
what people knew about him since this knowledge acted as a mirror
allowing Goethe to gain a clearer idea about himself and what lay
within him. This principle applies to brands, products and services,
but the mechanism is not as simple as just looking at what others
think and feel. The questions which are asked in market research
are always grounded in a philosophical foundation based on how we
construct reality, and a good researcher will make the assumptions
and theoretical framework for the research explicit. But when it
comes to the way in which we construct ideas about ourselves, who
we are and how we are perceived, the theoretical frameworks are
largely hidden in the depths of our consciousness.

The last chapter looked at the essential role that an authentic
purpose plays in developing customer experiences with soul. This

chapter looks at the barriers that are in place which can block our access to a deeper purpose, the principle barriers being ego, jealousy, insecurity, greed and status. When we are stuck in a purely analytical mode of cognition, we experience other people only as separate from us, and this results in many forms of counterproductive and dysfunctional behaviour.

While technology has allowed us to become more connected than ever before, social networking has resulted in us being under ever more pressure to present ourselves as key opinion formers and experts, as traditional models of permanent employment with corporations give way to people becoming multifaceted independently employed consultants, makers, artists and sharers. This is leading, ironically, not only to more collaboration, but also to increased competition, creating pressures which can impact on our ability to maintain coherence between saying, doing and meaning. When there is dissonance between what we say, what we do and how we act, we are perceived as counterfeit, and this is particularly true in the way in which we are perceived by people who are not our customers.

The essence of who you are fully comes to presence in the customer experience of those who are not your customers. You really get to experience the dynamics of someone's true purpose when they are interacting with people who are not their clients, or people who they perceive as adding no material benefits either to their business or social lives. When dealing with other people in any situation relating to either sharing, cooperating or collaborating these are important interactions to pay attention to, especially if you are extremely attentive to the giveaway 'tells' – the body language that poker players pay attention to and which reveal what a person is really thinking.

The journey from where we are now to developing customer experiences with soul starts with ourselves and our relationships with those immediately around us. If we can comprehend, understand and heal these broken and inauthentic relationships, then we can start to rediscover trust, values and what it means to genuinely share and co-create whatever we are attempting to envision, innovate and bring into this world. Across all organisations we find the same patterns which can be classified into a number of archetypal behaviours covering a spectrum from negative to positive. The dysfunctional ones prevent teams, departments, business units, divisions and businesses working together as a coherent whole.

Take a few moments to think about your daily conversations at work. Which ones are truly satisfying? Which are the conversations you have where you can honestly say that people recognise who you are, what you are truly able to bring to the conversation, and where there is full attention and genuine listening? Sometimes it can feel as if we are having conversations with our backs to each other. So take time to look at which conversations you are having where there is very little attention from the other person or people. This will help you to identify when one or more archetypal behaviours are operating, which interventions are required to resolve the negative ones, and which interventions are required to encourage the positive ones.

The first archetype is *predatory* behaviour. This is where a person cannot see, does not want to see, and refuses to see another person as they really are. They are unable to acknowledge skills, values and qualities within others, even though they do see that another person may have something of value to them. They see colleagues, partners, co-workers, subordinates and acquaintances as diminished, unimportant and weak. Predators view 'collaboration' as an opportunity to abuse and take advantage of people volunteering their free time, ideas and resources. This archetype can be quite a 'wolf in sheep's clothing', and can often be found in the sustainability community, where questions of ego, insecurity and jealousy still run rampant.

For those people who are politically adept and who do not have a fully developed sense of values and ethics, the sharing economy has resulted in new opportunities to exploit the goodwill and knowledge of others under the guise of collaboration and co-creation. One tactic is to ask someone to volunteer their time and energy in the name of a good cause, with a view to commercially and selfishly exploiting the output generated. Should those who are asked to contribute not wish to for whatever reason, it is possible to paint them in a negative light, rather than addressing the more fundamental causes as to why a particular co-creation project is not achieving the participation or success expected.

Whereas the predatory archetype is aggressive and calculated, the *blinkered* archetype is more tragic, and represents wasted opportunity and an inability to prosper by recognising those who are in their immediate circles. The blinkered mode is one of not valuing, questioning or showing interest in another person, and therefore either assuming or concluding that the person is not of value. This is a great archetype to introduce when working with leaders who often are unable to see the qualities, skills, knowledge and potential of people in their teams, thereby failing to maximise opportunities, projects and visions. It is not without reason that the first four chapters of *Holonomics* is devoted to the 'dynamics of seeing', and that we say that to see well is an act of humility. With humility, a whole new dimension of the world opens up; it's a powerful quality for leaders to develop.

The next archetype, *ego-trapped*, can be seen in people who you are having close conversations with. Reading their body language and examining the quality of eye contact reveals much about their inner mental life; trapped in their egos they are unable to see, or not mindful of how they are acting and what they are saying is revealing their true feelings. People who are ego-trapped have great difficulty in sharing the success of others, a dynamic which can hinder the development and execution of great ideas, projects and solutions. So one aspect of behaviour which leaders in innovative organisations need to nurture and develop is the ability of all team members to authentically share other people's achievements.

The ego-trapped archetype can particularly come to the fore in gurus, resulting in what we term 'guru-itus'. This syndrome results

descernment, holonomic

in mindfulness gurus who are not mindful, ethics gurus who are not ethical, dialogue gurus who cannot have a dialogue – the list is endless. The original meaning of 'guru' related to a person who was able to raise our essence and bring out the best in ourselves, but business gurus are often the opposite, creating an idea which becomes codified, packaged and then sold to people as *the* solution to their problems. Everyone's transformational journey has no start and no end, it is a lifetime of dedication. When we are discerning, educated and questioning, it becomes possible to see who is suffering from guru-itus, those people who have not actually had either such original or profound insights which they claim to have had.

 The next archetype, *discernment*, is all about non-judgement. This archetype is all about taking the plank out of one's own eye before trying to remove the speck of dust out of someone else's. When we are discerning, we can see with open eyes when someone is being a bit of an idiot, and in these instances often it is only a true friend who has the ability to point it out to them. This archetype is able to see through the more superficial appearance of someone's behaviours, who that person appears to be in that present moment, and is able to see the potential in that person and who they can become. It is important to practise discernment, because at times we do have to protect ourselves from the potentially destructive and hurtful actions of others, which diminish our energy levels and steal our enthusiasm and vitality, which we need to reach our goals and visions.

 The final archetype is *holonomic*, where we reach the stage of true dialogue, wholeness, authenticity, human values and an expansion of consciousness which allows us to see and know people as they truly are. People reach this archetype have battled their egos, been able to suspend their judgement, and have opened themselves to a new dynamic way of seeing. This allows them to value others, dissolve tensions, nurture authentic conversations full of emergent creativity, allowing themselves and those around them to live more happy and fulfilling lives.

These archetypes refer to issues and problems which can be

extremely difficult to address in an organisational setting. If we run away from these issues, the processes, methodologies and tools that we are working with will not have the expected results which they promise. In addition to examining these archetypes at the level of the individual, we also have to examine issues relating to working in teams and networks, since customer experiences with soul are never the result of just one person, but result from everyone working together in an organisation as an authentic whole.

Knotworks – Networks with Ego

As we move into our networked age, we hear a lot about co-creation, the collaborative economy, the networked economy, conscious in- novation and conscious capitalism. However, simply introducing words like 'co-creation', 'network' and 'collaborative' is not enough. The reason is ego, and it is ego which results in counterfeit *knotworks* instead of authentic *networks*.

The move from 'ego' to 'eco' is not simple. We have to lose a huge number of preconceptions about reality. It is our ego which sees the world and everything in it as separate from us. The fact that we see other people as separate from us can often lead to feelings of fear. The fear comes when we are not confident about ourselves, and when we fear others having what we do not have, because they are superior in some way. Ego is fuelled by our insecurities, and when we act from a position of distorted ego, sometimes all that we know how to do is to attack others, bring them down, destroy their reputations and show how we are superior.

Humility is one of the most powerful personal qualities we can possess. When we are humble, we have an ability to see. We are able see more, literally. We see the patterns, the causes, the motivations and ego which drives a person's behaviour, patterns which sometimes they themselves cannot see or are not aware of. When all our actions and desires come from an expanded level of consciousness, we act from a place that has the desire to benefit the whole – a whole group, a whole team, a whole family, a whole organisation, a whole tribe, a whole society, a whole planet. Solutions to the complex problems we face today are often so wicked that we do need authentic co-creation, dialogue, networks, and we need everyone contributing their very best to the whole. We need to be innovative, but sometimes all our efforts seem in vain, our ideas are rejected before being considered and our grand visions come to nothing. Why? It is because what we thought was a network is in fact a *knotwork*.

Knotworkers are those people who disrupt our disruption. We have to be careful with knotworkers, and ensure that we can detect them and know when their actions are likely to be destructive rather than constructively disruptive. We have to watch out for those knot-workers who talk the talk but in fact whose actions and motivations come from hierarchical thinking, from a desire to hold on to power and status, who plagiarise and steal others' work, never acknowledging their sources, and who are threatened by others. Many of us have believed in other people, shared our knowledge, only to have it stolen from us rather than being offered opportunities to collaborate and co-create. We have to watch out for this, as this is a part of reality, hence the need for discernment at all times.

It is not just data, information and knowledge which flows through social networks, but narratives. People motivated by power can therefore control a network through narratives which support their views of reality and sow false stories which they wish to impose on others through command-and-control. Platitudes such as the need to move from competition to collaboration have to be examined closely and the intention of the speaker detected, not just from the words uttered, since those who speak about collaboration may still have a competition mindset, and therefore still be using and abus-ing the power of narratives in order to exclude others who for some reason they may feel threatened.

Handwritten margin notes: "peace, truth, love, righteousness and non-violence." "Holonomic – thinking, sensing, feeling, intuition. 4 ways of knowing" "seeing"

One characteristic which distinguishes knotworks from authentic networks is the presence of cliques, small groups who use the language of sharing and community, but who still operate from hidden agendas and self-interest. Facebook did not suddenly turn us into yogis, monks, angels and saints. There is a big difference between social networks, communities and cultures. Communities may have the appearance and structure of social networks, but the outcome when they are inauthentic is the continuation of fragmentation in society. Neither an authentic purpose nor social networks on their own are able to develop customer experiences with soul. Networks must have more than shared values, as cliques do; they need to share the universal human values of peace, truth, love, righteousness and non-violence. When these values are present, and absolutely lived by each and every member, then communities develop a culture which reaches their highest potential, and enables the experience of soul to emerge.

Creativity, Ego and Transformational Leadership

Our work at Holonomics Education is centred around working with executives and people from many different business backgrounds, helping them to shift into a higher cognitive mode of operating – 'holonomic thinking'. Holonomic thinking is a mode of consciousness which utilises all four ways of knowing – thinking, sensing, feeling and intuition – and this mental operating system can apply equally to the way in which we understand brands and brand value.[21] When you go into the act of 'seeing', you develop a sensitivity to the lived experience of others, a powerful ability which leads to comprehension, empathy and an understanding of the motives, actions and underlying causes of the outwardly perceived actions and expressions of other people. Reaching this deeper way of seeing requires people to develop higher organs of perception, and these can only be developed by embarking on a journey of personal transformation. This journey is the transition of consciousness.

Nigel Hoffmann's work examines the role that artistic capabilities play in comprehending the dynamic, living qualities of nature.[22] Inspired by his work, we created a very simple four elements of thinking framework which we use to help our clients and students contemplate the different modes of consciousness which we can experience in the creative and transformative stages we must pass through in the development and elevation of our ways of knowing and understanding reality. Each mode is essential and no single mode is more important than another; certain situations require one way of thinking more than the others. Each mode of consciousness is associated with the different qualities of each element:

Earth: solid objects, grounding, know where you stand, finding common ground, standing your ground, discrete entities, hard, motionless, measurable, countable, well-defined.

Water: fluidity, flow, transparent, moving around objects, looser meanings, formless, continuous, process, feelings.

Air: inspiration, gesture, musical, spaciousness, flying, single mass, creative, expansion in all directions.

Fire: transformation, transition, alchemy, change, creation, energy, creative impulse, intuition, poetical, coming-into-being of living form.

Earth thinking is our every day three-dimensional mechanical thinking. This mode of thinking is an absolute necessity in allowing us to navigate our world which we experience in four dimensions – three directions and time – even though quantum physics tells us that our world is quite the opposite of how we imagine it to be. The earth thinking modality is one of solidity, solid concepts; it is the world in which we are grounded, reassuringly familiar, predictable, controllable and knowable. Many people are so comfortable and rooted in this way of knowing reality that they are unable to engage in any meaningful dialogue, being so sure of the 'facts', and that their version of 'reality' is the true one and nothing else possibly could be.

When we engage in dialogue, we move into a more fluid way of thinking, the *water* mode. Our concepts become less fixed as we realise that we may have significant things to learn from others, and we are therefore able to adapt our concepts as we take on the alternative perspectives and points of view. Conversations flow when barriers are removed, such as our certainty in our own beliefs, and when we have a genuine desire to learn, developing our abilities to listen without judgement.

Air is much lighter than water, and when we transform our thinking again we are able to achieve ever higher levels of inspiration, sometimes without truly understanding where this inspiration comes from. In yoga and other spiritual practices there are many breathing exercises which are used to calm the mind and achieve a deeper level of mindfulness. Air thinking is not bounded by limitations or restrictions, concepts collide and fuse in a heightened level of creativity and insight.

Fire is the element of transformation. Just as we are scared of fire as it can burn us, our subconscious can hold us back from entering into fire thinking due to fear of the dissolution of ego. We cannot transform ourselves with this mode of thinking unless we can leave our prior selves behind, and accordingly many people are unable to take this step into fire. Fire lies beyond air, since we no longer separate that which we observe and attempt to comprehend from ourselves. It is only by entering fire that there is an alchemical transformation enabling us to reach a depth of profound comprehension which previously eluded us.

As well as there being a journey of outward transformation – earth, water, air, fire – there is also an return path of grounding – fire, air, water, earth – where we take the insights gained from an expanded level of consciousness and awareness and begin to craft these insights into inspirational ideas, which we then prototype, and then implement back in our familiar sensory world in which we live. This journey of transformation is one of creative insight and will be familiar to many designers and other creative people, including leaders who manage to reach a sufficient degree of mastery allowing them to shift into experiencing states of flow. However, there are certain traps which block the path to achieving mastery, traps which we do need to address and which are not often talked about since they address our shadow selves, that side of us which we rarely wish to look at, analyse and resolve.

The first trap is to confuse academic or intellectual comprehension with intuitive insight. The next big advance in leadership and management will come when we stop confusing the codification of reality with our experience of life. When we codify reality, we develop frameworks, flow charts and classification systems. If this is done mindfully, when the conscious awareness that what we are creating are constructive conceptions and not dogmatic annunciations, then we can offer people new ways of seeing which will lead to genuine insights which do speak meaningfully about reality. Understanding the limitations of codification – especially the limitations of linear and hierarchical codified models of 'consciousness' – opens the door to an expansion of consciousness.

The second trap is one of being caught up in our egos. This journey is one from 'ego-centric' consciousness to 'eco-centric' consciousness. Many leaders, especially in the West, have become leaders through ego-centric consciousness not just of themselves, but of a society which rewards ego-centric behaviour. In our new reality 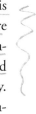 which is emerging and being co-created, this is no longer working, but there are still people who are not actually aware that they are acting from a place of ego. When you do fully live the five universal human values you become more aware of the underlying dynamics and causes of people's surface behaviours and actions, and you are more aware of how your own actions may be perceived by others.

A great danger exists in that we may believe that we have reached the fire stage when we have not. We may still be threatened by others (ego), as opposed to recognising who they really are and seeing how they can contribute, co-create and belong to an authentic whole (eco). This is an extremely difficult lesson for those already in leadership and high-status positions, probably one of the hardest lessons of all.

The third trap exists within the fire stage, when on reaching this level of transformation, you are so affected by the transformation that you do not know what to do with the insights. Fire burns, and so people on this journey need to be prepared for it. It also very much shows us why we need mentors, guides and authentic facilitators to hold the space for us and then to guide us out of the fire and back onto the return journey.

The fourth trap is one where you reach the stage of fire, of transformation, but you get so blown away by the depth of insight that you then attempt to articulate yourself from here. This is a huge lesson for leaders, since in order to inspire, you have to be able to address people at the level of their conscious awareness, and not your own. The solution to this trap is to realise that the journey is not one-way; you have to buy yourself a return ticket when you set out, returning through the very stages you came through on your way. When we become able to both see the world with new eyes and still relate to those others who have not yet passed through this level of transformation, we are able to modify the way we communicate and talk about concepts which speak of a higher purpose and more soulful experiences.

An authentic leader must walk this journey, and no shortcuts are available. You cannot study your way through this journey gathering ever more codified knowledge; it has to be experiential. Those leaders who are capable of developing organisations which deliver customer experiences with soul have found a balance in the four ways of knowing and fully utilise all of their faculties of knowing; thinking, feeling, sensing and intuition (Figure 3). We call these four ways of knowing the 'holonomic operating system'.[23] *Holonomics* explores this mental operating system in depth, explaining what this means both for our own ways of understanding the world, and also in terms of the implications for the design, implementation and communication of customer experiences with soul and of sustainable brands.

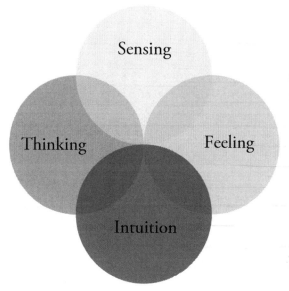

Figure 3: The Four Ways of Knowing

Although neuroscientists have understood that the brain was not divided into a rational side and an emotional side since the early 1980s, people today still believe this to be true. The brain is divided, and the two hemispheres do operate in profoundly different ways, but not as we realise.[24] The left hemisphere provides instrumental attention. This allows us to manipulate objects and use things for our benefit. But this type of attention is narrowly focused, and it means that we experience reality as fragmented, static and ultimately lifeless. It is the right hemisphere that provides what one might call relational attention, enabling us to see the whole picture, to form social bonds, and to inhabit and belong to the world we see, rather than simply being detached from it and merely using it.

However, we have become out of balance, and our thinking has become dominated by the left brain way of seeing, especially in Western economies. In the modern business world, dominated by technology, 'thinking' is valued above all other ways of knowing the world. This is the logical, rational and symbolic way of thinking which gives us a sense of separation from the world. Note here that 'feeling' is opposite 'thinking'. 'Feeling' here is not emotion. It is through 'feeling' that we achieve a sense of connection to other people and to nature. 'Sensing' is the way of knowing of artists, photographers, painters and chefs. Whereas sensory knowing is very concrete, intuition provides us with a much deeper sense of the meaning of phenomena. It is responsible for insights, scientific discoveries and new ways of seeing. Discovering the four ways of knowing can be extremely powerful, especially for business executives who may be really stuck in 'thinking'. If we can find this level of authenticity inside ourselves, we will be able to make a huge impact in both our companies, organisations and brands, and our communities in which we live and work. The reason is that our own personal customer experiences, the experiences people have of us, will be more authentic and more soulful.

So far we have discussed the trinity of saying, doing and meaning which are at the centre of the holonomic circle, and this chapter has described some of the dysfunctional behaviours and organisational characteristics which act as barriers to people being able to work together in harmonious coherent networks. The next chapter introduces tools and techniques, the middle layer of the holonomic circle which consists of the five principles of purpose, methods, relationships, meaning and human values. These principles elucidate the underlying dynamics of soulful experiences, and therefore provide the guidance needed for developing, structuring and implementing customer experiences with soul.

4. The Holonomic Circle –
Tools and Techniques

Designing the Customer Experience

BT Group has had an interesting history in the UK. In 1912, the British General Post Office was given the monopoly to build the UK's telecoms infrastructure. British Telecom was formed in 1980 and became independent from the Post Office in 1981, and then was privatised in 1984, with 50% of the shares being sold to investors. The second half of British Telecom was sold in 1991 and 1993, which coincided with Simon joining the group in 1992 as a psychologist in BT's Human Factors Department, within its research department at BT Laboratories, which also contained the Speech Recognition and Futurology departments, headed up by Peter Cochrane, one of the UK's leading futurologists.

Along with Xerox PARC, the BT Human Factors team was one of the largest in the world, and unlike more academic teams based in universities, members worked extremely closely with their marketing colleagues, who were the department's internal clients. In 1995 Simon co-authored a paper with Mike Atyeo *Delivering Competitive Edge*, writing:

> Usability is a key business driver and user-centred techniques are emerging to deliver this competitive edge. It is essential to move away from simple product design, beyond

the integrated service design of product, packaging, documentation, and after-sales service, to the comprehensive design of the customer experience.

In response to rapid technological change and increased global competition, service industries have undergone radical change. These were initially focused on reducing cost and time to market, but more recently have concentrated on ways of understanding and anticipating customer needs. We have adopted an approach we call 'designing the customer experience'. At its heart was a programme of research into human needs. By bringing together Marketing and Human Factors with more radical perspectives such as semiotics and anthropology, creative and visualisation skills, and rapid technological advances, we have generated an environment for user-centred innovation.[25]

We express users' abilities, needs and preferences from psychological and ergonomic perspectives, matched to demographic, lifestyle, economic and other marketing factors. Our approach takes a multi-perspective view of customers and users and provides clear roles for multiple disciplines to work together to deliver the competitive edge of usability.

One of the key success factors for the Human Factors team was the quality of the relationships they were developing with their colleagues at BT Marketing who understood the value of their work and gave them considerable support. By developing a common understanding, they were able to position Human Factors in the very earliest stages of the product lifecycle, allowing product marketing managers to refine ideas while still at the concept stage, thus saving the disproportionate amount of effort, time and cost which could

have been necessary to re-work the products later in the development process. Their tools and techniques included:

Concept evaluation: a rapid impact analysis, designed to provide a 'first cut' analysis of costs, timescales and issues.

Usage scenarios: designed to communicate the concept.

Initial concept testing: the use of focus groups to gain an early understanding of users' attitudes and likely acceptance.

Early prototyping: includes task-based product interaction as well as discussion, providing qualitative behavioural data in addition to subjective response data.

Field trials: These are tests done with more advanced prototypes, allowing people to try the products and services in their normal daily environments rather than artificial environments such as a usability laboratory.

The motivation for writing both this paper and a subsequent paper *Working with Marketing* (co-authored with Mike Atyeo, Charanjit Sidhu and Gerry Coyle)[26] was that human factors was still a nascent discipline, with user-centred design still being mainly concerned with human computer interaction. The majority of user-interface design experts were still based in universities and technical research centres, and as such there was little meaningful dialogue with people in marketing departments in commercial businesses. The approach taken at BT was to develop a multi-perspective view of customers which provided a clear role for multiple disciplines to work together, expressing users' abilities, needs and preferences from psychological and ergonomic perspectives, and matching these with demographic, lifestyle, economic, and other marketing factors.

In the last twenty years, design thinking has come to take a dominant position in product and service design, although it has as its basis the approach to designing the customer experience which came from a wide range of disciplines including human factors, user interface design, marketing, psychology, anthropology, ethnography. Design thinking has been complemented with advances in the approach to the development of business models and value propositions, with canvasses enabling a shared language for describing, visualising and evolving products and services.

The middle level of the holonomic circle helps us to think about those factors which underlie these tools and techniques, and also to help us understand why they sometimes work and why at times they do not (Figure 4). This layer is not about telling you which tools and techniques to use. It is about exploring the underlying foundations of the tools and techniques being used and seeing which principles need to be operating in order that the tools and techniques become more effective.

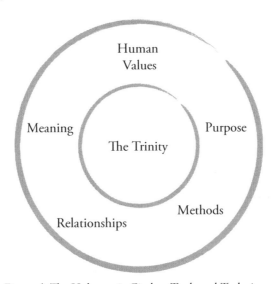

Figure 4: The Holonomic Circle – Tools and Techniques

As a human factors specialist at BT Laboratories Simon already had three years training as a psychologist. As a practitioner doing experiments and studies with members of the public he had to comply with the ethical guidelines of the British Psychological Society, and rightly so. When carrying out experiments and usability trials with people, there are many aspects which can adversely affect their emotions, and at BT there were many experimental designs that had to be rejected which, although they could have given more accurate results, could have potentially resulted in participants thinking that perhaps there was something wrong with them, as opposed to the design of the interface being testing.

In addition to the ethical aspects, psychological experiments are also carefully designed to avoid extraneous factors being introduced accidentally, such as some behaviour from the experimenter which may bias the results and so produce false conclusions. With the explosion of popularity in design thinking, people are now being encouraged to copy the tools and techniques of designers after simply taking part in a course which may only last for few days. A third type of bias which can adversely impact on the quality of a design thinking process is the bias and hidden agendas of those researchers who may be looking simply to confirm an existing hypothesis, or who may wish to use design thinking and other co-creation methods for political reasons, to obtain buy-in and acceptance for a new project or initiative.

These different forms of bias and manipulation result from the archetypal behaviours we saw in chapter three, and also from knotworks where cliques within an organisation may wish to extend their political power and status. Tools and techniques therefore can be used by people who are operating from different levels of consciousness and with different values. This chapter will now explore purpose, methods, relationships, meaning and human values in order to show how these operate to help an organisation come together as a whole to elevate its value propositions, business models, products and services to the level of customer experiences with soul.

Purpose

In his book *Disrupted: My Misadventure in the Start-Up Bubble*, Dan Lyon makes some devastating observations from an insider's point of view of his year inside the hi-tech startup HubSpot.[27] His principal observation was that HubSpot started out as a sales operation in search of a product, meaning that the first people to be hired included a head of sales and a head of marketing. The implicit purpose of startups is therefore to scale quickly and become large rather than profitable. We could call this the antithesis of authentic purpose, where a startup is created with the explicit purpose of purely making money. Indeed, Lyon explains how he feels that there has been a shift from a focus on the product to a focus on the business model, with the idea of creating new technology which solves a genuine need being secondary.

This approach to launching a startup is the polar opposite to BrewDog who were clear from the very beginning that their mission was to "make people as passionate about great beer as we are" together with an "overarching ambition to be the best possible employer in the world". In order to grow, BrewDog do two things. The first is to be relentless in their efforts to develop new world-class craft beers. The second is to invest heavily in training, describing their people as "the heart and soul of the company" who "live and breathe our culture". In 2016 BrewDog achieved a level of sustained growth resulting in an organisation of 650 people, shipping beer to over 60 countries and operating 30 BrewDog bars in the UK and 47 globally.[28]

For four years in a row, from 2012 to 2015, they were the fastest growing food and drinks company in the UK. With their trajectory for growth set to continue into 2016 and 2017, they decided to articulate more formally their culture through a collaborative process, polling 400 BrewDog staff and then distilling the essence of their culture down into the following five points in focus groups with the twenty longest-standing employees:

We Bleed Craft Beer
– This is our true north.

We are Uncompromising
– If we don't love it, we don't do it. Ever.

We Blow Shit Up
– We are ambitious. We are relentless. We take risks.

We are Geeks
– Learn obsessively. Share evangelically.

Without Us, We are Nothing
– We. Are. BrewDog.

In October 2015 James Watt put together a seven page internal memo and distributed it to every BrewDog employee. He described the charter as their bible for decision-making, a way in which their growing organisation could continue to make decisions "in a BrewDog way". The document was not intended to cover everything BrewDog did; it was written "just to help our team make decisions and implement the charter". The charter contains the essential essence and spirit of BrewDog, and it is therefore a great lesson in reminding leaders that it is never simply enough to develop an authentic purpose; a company must always return to its purpose regularly to review it, update it if necessary, and continually evangelise it throughout the whole organisation.

An example of the radical mission of BrewDog, and their commitment to craft beer can be seen in their extremely surprising gesture to the global community of home brewers in February 2016 when they published on line the recipes to every single one of the beers that they had ever produced. The initiative was called DIY Dog, with every recipe sheet containing all the information that would allow home brewers to clone the beer at home. Watt explained DIY Dog as their way of giving something back to the community:

> We have always loved the sharing of knowledge, expertise and passion in the craft beer community and we wanted to take that spirit of collaboration to the next level. With DIY Dog we wanted to do something that has never been done before as well as paying tribute to our home-brewing roots. We wanted to take all of our recipes, every single last one, and give them all away for free, to the amazing global home-brewing community.[29]

The leadership at the top of the organisation must never become complacent, and must develop strong relationships with everyone in the business, in order that each and every person truly understands the meaning of the purpose in a way which will inspire and uplift them. In this manner it becomes possible to develop customer experiences with soul, which can be seen as a result of the heart and soul that each person puts in to their work.

Albert Borgman holds the position of Regents Professor Emeritus of Philosophy at the University of Montana. He tells his students, "you can't buy the meaning of life, you can't borrow it and you can't manufacture it. You can only discover it." Every so often invites his students to search their experiences, hopes and aspirations for occasions where they are in the position to affirm four propositions:[30]

> There is no place I would rather be.
> There is no one I would rather be with.
> There is nothing I would rather be doing.
> This I will remember well.

These are four potent propositions that we need in order to determine whether our lives really are being lived authentically, on a foundation of a deeper purpose, or whether we are still looking to find our authentic selves. When we are acting authentically we are more fully able to confront the 'slings and arrows of outrageous fortune' in our lives, being more fully equipped to confront any challenging situation in which we may find ourselves, situations which may be unique or which we have never personally encountered before. Authenticity fires us in times of trouble, keeping us resolute, providing us with our true north. We can learn a lot about how to respond to challenging situations from jazz musicians who over many years learn how to respond by always being fully present, connecting with their instruments, connecting with themselves, and connecting with every other musician playing in their ensemble.

Austin Peralta was a virtuoso jazz musician and composer who died at the tragically young age of 22 in 2012, a genuine musical prodigy who started to play the piano from the age of six. At school he observed the manner in which school teachers would talk to their students who they felt were not playing correctly. The key component missing in school music lessons was the ability to listen to other musicians:

> What's lacking is listening to everyone else in the room and understanding that I don't have to rely on just everything I already know. If I listen to the other guys at the moment I can come up with new things on the spot. With jazz I don't even take note of what I am doing or what I am playing, I just think about what is going on in that moment with the other musicians and this is what I am bringing. It's really hard to describe.[31]

Authenticity combined with active listening can therefore allow us to take risks. For jazz trumpeter Jumanee Smith, taking risks is an essential part of jazz:

> Improvisation is supposed to be the element of freedom entering into space that hasn't been seen before. You are supposed to always be trying something new instead of playing patterns or playing something that everybody has heard before.[32]

One of the main reasons why Judith was driving Fábio stir crazy as he was attempting to cancel his phone contract (chapter one) was that she was doggedly sticking to a pre-determined rule-driven script, one which prevented Judith's natural personality from shining through, and which, combined with the pressure of stressful and challenging sales targets, resulted in one of our most dreaded customer experiences – that of contacting a service provider's call centre. When sales and service staff in call centres are given a set of guiding principles rather than a set of prescribed actions, as we shall see in the following section, the experience for customers is transformed.

Methods

In many company cultures we can see that the inductive and analytical mindset is dominant. In these cultures, 'soft skills' are often seen in a derogatory or less important light than 'hard skills'. Thinking is the most important skill that we have in business today, but the majority of organisations fail to develop advanced thinking skills in high-performance leaders. The focus is on the products of thinking systems, and not on thought itself. The dimension of mind is continually missed in relation to thinking about seeing. We think that what we see is what everyone sees, but in fact all of us live in a world of lived experience, and this is independent of the sensory experience open to all of us.

Through experiential training we can learn to develop an expanded mode of consciousness, a deeper way of seeing which has monumental implications for creativity, communication, leadership, strategy, innovation, in fact every single dimension of organisational life. With this expanded level of consciousness the dichotomy between hard and soft begins to dissolve as the whole organisation shifts into a focus on the quality of relationships, developing a higher purpose, longevity, qualitative success metrics and a more systemic view of life.

Customer experiences with soul are found in organisations which are holonomic, where there is a balance between analytical and artistic consciousness. It is not that one form of consciousness is higher or more important than another; the key movement is an expansion of consciousness, allowing the whole organisation and the complete customer experience to be fully understood. We need to balance the more typical approach of abstraction of ideas with the ability to plunge into the experience of that which we wish to understand, and this includes living systems. This insight was articulated by Werner Karl Heisenberg (1901–1976) who was one of the key pioneers of quantum physics. In 1932 he gave a lecture to the Saxon Academy of Science in which rather than applauding the progress of science, he warned of the need for science to continually be aware of its own way of thinking in order that it continually evaluated the manner in which science developed an understanding of nature through the construction of laws:

> Almost every scientific advance is bought at the cost of renunciation, almost every gain in knowledge sacrifices important standpoints and established modes of thought. As facts and knowledge accumulate, the claim of the scientist to an understanding of the world in a certain sense diminishes.[33]

Francis Bacon (1561–1626) has been called the father of empiricism, famous for his writings on the scientific approach based on induction. This is where the scientist attempts to find many different cases and then tries to generalise from them. For example, an observation is made that one metal melts when heated. Two more observations of two more metals melting when heated are made. From these specific instances, it is deduced that all metals melt when heated. As a teacher of the history of science, Henri Bortoft pointed out that Bacon did not actually write that science worked in this way, and that he did not advocate the methods for which he is universally credited.[34] Bacon did include induction in his writings, saying the following:

> The induction of which the logicians speak, which proceeds by simple enumeration, is a puerile thing and leads to no result.[35]

This is quite remarkable. In Bacon's writing it is clear that he did not give all phenomena equal value. Bacon, in *Novum Organum*, singled out certain instances which are especially instructive. He emphasised what he called "the shining instances" or "the striking instances":

> Among Prerogative Instances I will put in the third place Striking Instances, of which I have made mention in the First Vintage Concerning Heat, and which I also call Shining Instances, or Instances Freed and Predominant. They are those which exhibit the nature in question naked and standing by itself, and also in its exaltation or highest degree of power; as being disenthralled and freed from all impediments, or at any rate by virtue of its strength dominant over, suppressing and coercing them.[36]

While Bacon referred to "shining instances", Goethe referred to "an instance worth a thousand bearing all within itself". It is interesting therefore to see that initially Goethe admired the philosophy of Bacon, regarding him as an authority on scientific method, and basing his own ideas on how to do science on those of Bacon. In his later years Goethe changed his attitude to Bacon, calling Bacon, "a Hercules... who cleanses a stable of dialectical dung, only to let it fill up with empirical dung".[37]

Towards the end of his life Goethe dictated some notes on Bacon, saying:

> In the range of phenomena all had equal value in Bacon's eyes. For although he himself always points out that one should collect the particulars only to select from them and to arrange them, in order finally to attain to Universals, yet too much privilege is granted to the single facts; and before it becomes possible to attain to simplification and conclusion by means of induction (the very way he recommends), life vanishes and forces get exhausted. He who cannot realise that one instance is often worth a thousand, bearing all within itself; he who proves unable to comprehend and esteem what we called ur-phenomena, will never be in a position to advance anything, either to his own or to others' joy and profit.[38]

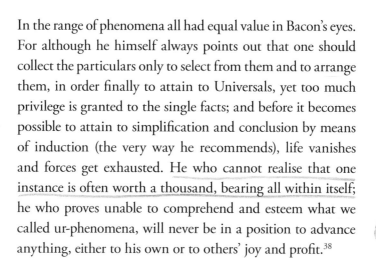

Henri saw "shining instances" as being the same idea as "an instance worth a thousand bearing all within itself" from which all secondary factors have fallen away. In his writings Bacon did not give all phenomena equal value, giving too much privilege to single facts. Henri felt that Goethe had managed to do what Bacon wanted to do but could not, pointing out that if something shines, what does it do? It shines, it appears. In Henri's words, "the idea appears in the phenomenon".[39]

The phrase "an instance worth a thousand bearing all within itself" is a key concept for Goethe. It shows that Goethe's way of proceeding is phenomenological and not just empirical. To understand

Allegory / true poetry

wholeness in systems is to understand the dynamic relationship between the whole and the parts. In order to reach this level of understanding, we have to understand the coming-into-being of phenomena, be they phenomena organisms, brands, works of art, written texts, or business organisations. Once we have a deeper experience of meaning, then our level of consciousness changes and we become more alive and responsive to all that is alive and responsive in our environment. Henri used the example of triangles to help us understand how we can reverse our understanding of the universal and the particular:

The relationship between the universal and the particular is somewhat different for Goethe; he turns it inside out. We see the universal shining through the particular. The particular is seen 'universally'. In the usual relationship it is not like this at all, because the particular is just seen as an instance of the universal, for example, triangles. When you draw a triangle, the triangle is just seen as an instance of the universal triangle. You don't have this experience with that one triangle, you see the essence of triangularity shining through it. What happens is that you see each triangle simply as an instance of the universal. Goethe developed a different kind of scientific method whereby we come to the universal through the particular. In empirical science we lose the particular. Goethe is working in a poetic way.[40]

The ability to develop an artistic level of consciousness should not be undervalued and it should not be seen as a 'soft' skill. Through the contemplation of poetry we can begin to develop an understanding of the difference between allegory and what Goethe called "true poetry":

There is a great difference between a poet seeking the particular for the universal, and seeing the universal in the particular. The one gives rise to Allegory, where the particular serves only as instance or example of the general; but the

other is the true nature of Poetry, namely, the expression of the particular without any thought of, or reference to, the general. If a man grasps the particular vividly, he also grasps the general, without being aware of it at the time; or he may make the discovery long afterwards.[41]

We can start to understand this by imagining that we are reading a poem about an encounter between a man and a woman. The poem is not just about that particular man and woman, which of course it is, but it is about that particular encounter between a man and a woman raised to the universal, because something universal shines through the particular case.[42] The particular case is what it is, but it is illuminated by the universal which it illuminates. This is different to allegory, where the universal and particular are separate, and where the particular is used simply to illustrate the universal. Allegory was used a great deal in poetry, such as Spencer's *Faerie Queene* which look at what each thing represents. This is not the same as seeing the universal *through* the particular. Artistic consciousness, therefore, can help us to develop a more nuanced way of analysing complexity, especially in relation to the human condition. An interesting example is provided by phenomenologist Erazim Kohák in his analysis of jealousy in Othello:

> For example, the self-reinforcing pattern of jealousy is not accidental; it has a structurally necessary 'logic' of its own, which we grasp rather than deduce or construct. When, however, we seek to grasp it in an actual experience, it is often obscured by a myriad of contingent factors. An empirical report of the observed behaviour of the commanding officer of the Venetian armed forces, his wife and his chief of staff would yield a cumbersome mass a trivia about the life of military officers and their dependents. Shakespeare's fictional

account of Othello cuts through all of that presenting the pure *eidos* of the complex phenomenon jealousy.[43]

This approach analyses jealousy from a phenomenological perspective, in which jealousy is 'seen' directly. Henri expanded on Kohák's approach in the following way:

> Jealousy has a logic of its own which we can grasp. When we do grasp this, we see it, we do not infer it. We don't deduce it, we do not speculate. We can see jealousy directly. In many cases of jealousy, there will be a myriad of factors which will not be important. You want to find 'an instance worth a thousand bearing all' and Kohák finds this in Othello.
>
> Othello is an instance in a thousand bearing all within itself. The fact that it is present in the imaginative mode of consciousness instead of in the perceptual mode of consciousness, as actual experience, doesn't make any difference to its phenomenological function. If you were to try to find out what jealousy is in an empirical manner, you would just simply get bogged down in the irrelevant details of people's lives.[44]

By complementing an empirical approach to product and service design with this phenomenological approach, we can discover that on occasions what makes the difference between a good experience and an exceptional experience, which can often be found in one small detail. For example, no matter how good the other aspects of a hotel may be, one detail which can leave a lasting impression is the feeling we get from starting our day with a great cup of coffee. This may seem like a trivial point, but there is something significant to learn about customer experience design. Sometimes we can find a phenomenon, such as the coffee in a hotel, which contains the whole

archetypal experiences V's
less archetypal experiences

essence of the brand, the company, the values, the experience as a whole; and when we find this archetypal experience, it is worth a thousand less archetypal experiences.

When we moved to São Paulo in 2012 we did have the use of a small weights room in our condominium, which although adequate was extremely limited, leading us to join a new gym just around the corner called Mockba. The philosophy of the gym takes its inspiration from physical training techniques developed in Russia, hence the Russian inspired name and branding. Bruno Tripoli, the founder of Mockba, introduced us to the gym, telling us how it focuses not just on offering the traditional weight training equipment, but also offers more hardcore training programmes such as throwing around extremely large tractor tyres etc. All the staff are welcoming, friendly and attentive and there are always two or three trainers on hand at any time, putting together programmes and demonstrating the exercises. Although this does sound like the same way that other gyms operate, this is not always the case, with a friend of ours receiving no attention at all after falling off a running machine at her own gym. In focusing on the customer experience, an organisation has to have coherent values at the heart of its thinking, and this thinking has to run authentically throughout each and every aspect, and each and every member of staff.

Having staff who are not glued to their smart phones in a service context is an 'instance worth a thousand bearing all within itself', and at Mockba the staff are constantly attentive, keeping an eye out for you if they see you doing something slightly wrong, coming up and making the necessary corrections so that you do not accidentally hurt or strain yourself. This level of attention is hard to achieve for service organisations and comes from people who themselves understand the true value and meaning of service. Before developing the gym, Bruno told us that he had read the biography of Steve Jobs, and he really took notice of the way in which Jobs described the attention given to the experience of opening an Apple product box.

pleasure.

Bruno applied this thinking to the design of the gym and every aspect of the customer experience, including attention to the height of the ceilings, leading him to finding the building in São Paulo where Mockba was founded in 2011.

Matt Watkinson is one of the world's most respected customer experience designers, and the author of the best-selling book *The Ten Principles Behind Great Customer Experiences* which was published in 2013. Watkinson wrote the book because, as a "doer" with many years of experience, he noticed that "we were increasingly focused on following processes and using very complex methods that weren't really translating into the results that we needed, and I believe that was because we were neglecting the basics of what makes for a great experience".[45]

While design conversations would focus on usability, examining factors such as stress and effort involved in tasks, more fundamental aspects of experience such as pleasure were being ignored. Watkinson felt that what was missing from the canon of design and customer experience methodologies was a set of simple guidelines that people could use which would always lead them towards making better decisions by helping them to structure their thinking. He developed the ten principles which could also help people interpret all the data and information that people already had.[46] The ten principles are:

1. Great customer experiences strongly reflect the customer's identity.
2. Great customer experiences satisfy our higher objectives.
3. Great customer experiences leave nothing to chance.
4. Great customer experiences set and then meet expectations.
5. Great customer experiences are effortless.
6. Great customer experiences are stress free.
7. Great customer experiences indulge the senses.
8. Great customer experiences are socially engaging.
9. Great customer experiences put the customer in control.

10. Great customer experiences consider the emotions.

In order to help put these principles into practice, Watkinson has developed ten worksheets which can be downloaded from his website, and these include both blank worksheets and worked examples.[47] Not only do these principles help make the decision making process easier, they also help to focus discussions around what you should do. Having the ten principles in mind allows designers to better identify exactly what the problems are that customers are having with the experiences which are being created; and knowing which questions to ask leads to better answers to inform the analysis. The principles are powerful because they enable people to really get behind the experiences that customers are having:

> My clients home in on problems more quickly, and they have a better way of interpreting all the other research and data which they have. So, for example, you may see a drop off at some point on your website, and you could spend a long time hypothesising why, but when you have a set of universal principles, you can ask questions such as is it something to do with effort, or something to do with error. Could it be to do with the fact that people expect one thing to happen, but something else is happening?[48]

Watkinson makes the point that the principles can be provided as guidelines for frontline staff who have direct contact with customers, enabling them to think about the ways in which they can improve their interactions and contact. The principles therefore help to unify people across teams, departments and businesses in a way in which more traditional command-and-control organisations struggle with, creating a more holistic and connected experience for customers.

In the 1980s and 1990s, the discipline design thinking was pioneered by Tim Brown and Roger Martin. This period saw a shift

map out the journey,
not focus on destination
a focus on outcomes missed all
this

from participatory design to placing the end user at the centre of the design process, and to more current service design processes which aim to map out the entire user journey and embrace a wider range of stakeholders. James Souttar is a designer and communication consultant who has a great personal interest in typography, type-design and Persian calligraphy. Like Simon, James was also a student of the philosopher Henri Bortoft, and we have enjoyed many conversations with James in relation to Henri's philosophy and how it relates to the design and development of customer experiences with soul:

The fundamental flaw with 'design thinking' is that it prioritises a perfected outcome over a fulfilling journey. This is giving us a world of constantly improved things which are yet strangely unsatisfying and increasingly inhuman in their perfection. The same thing applies even more to the application of design thinking outside of thing-making. For instance, we can design an improved customer experience, basing our design on careful research and testing. Everything about this experience can thus be improved, except that it is no longer an authentic human encounter. Approaching it as a design problem has robbed it of its soul. For instance, I am currently learning Persian calligraphy. We write with a sharpened reed, which is effectively a piece of stick. Looked at through the eyes of design thinking, this practice could be substantially improved – a designer could come back with a writing implement made, for instance, of a polymer, with a continuous ink supply, better handling, and so forth. The process could be made easier, with a view to producing better outcomes (easier practice, more polished and consistent results).

But in fact the greatest value of learning this style of calligraphy, for me, is what the learning process teaches me about myself, what goes on in the encounter with my teacher, what it means to stand before something that is quite alien and seemingly impossible and slowly to begin to make it part of oneself. A focus on outcomes misses all of this, going straight to the end result (and even treating experience as a 'thing'). It is a paradigmatic example of what Henri Bortoft called 'finished product thinking', missing completely the dimension of 'coming into being'. And if I wanted to produce 'perfect' calligraphy, I can do that on my computer with ever more sophisticated fonts – because someone has applied design thinking to the computerisation of pretty much everything. But I don't want to do that, because that experience is too easy, too lacking in meaning, and soulless.

This is an enlightening approach to design, since it focuses on the value of experience as a process, and it does not superficially focus on the final outcome. When we achieve mastery in a skill such as calligraphy, our experience qualitatively changes, taking us into the 'coming-into-being' of that which we are working on. Deepening our perception of the nature of things allows us to become more attuned and empathic to the situation or phenomena we are studying and it can help take us out of 'operative thinking' where we try and turn everything to our own advantage, including both nature and spirituality. James sees many dangers for brands which wish to develop customer experiences with soul but who only attempt to commoditise experience:

> I struggle with the idea of 'customer experiences' (or 'experience design') because when the connection between two people goes beyond the merely transactional, it leaves the transactional behind. When the barista is your friend, buying an espresso from him is an irrelevance. But if he tries to sell more espressos by 'putting soul into the experience', we're dealing with inauthentic experiences – "I'll pretend to be your friend,

so you buy more coffee from me". And there's a price to pay for that kind of prostitution. If it's a human experience, it has a human quality. It can be pleasant to buy from someone who is present and authentic, but unless the connection becomes something else (for instance, it develops into a friendship), it just remains a transaction. We can't use 'soul' like a chilli sauce to spice up an otherwise lacklustre commercial offer.

Part of the problem is that what's happening with brands is that they are trying to commoditise experience. And really, it's the only place left for brands to go. So there's an attempt to make more and more of the human aspects of a transaction subservient to the brand. "How can we change the behaviours of staff so that they are perceived as more personable, more engaging, more authentic – 'stickier' – without, of course, compromising their productivity?" The dilemma here – which goes to the heart of your question about what we mean by the word 'soul' – is that the qualities of warmth, empathy, attention, interaction etc. do enliven a transactional experience. But is it right to try to make these qualities subservient to the brand – to make 'soul' work for return on investment, shareholder value, and executive bonuses? Or is that a step too far?

When we develop a dynamic sense of the whole and the parts, it not longer becomes the case that 'soul' is subservient to the brand, for the brand itself is the outer articulation of an authentic purpose. Holonomic thinking enables us to comprehend how the soul and essence of a business or organisation expresses itself and comes to presence through each and every part. In order to see how brands can avoid the trap of developing an inauthentic sense of soul, we therefore now need to examine the nature of relationships between businesses and clients, the way in which 'meaning' can be derived jointly and the role that values play.

Relationships

In his 2003 Harvard Business Review article *The One Number You Need to Grow*, Fred Reichheld introduced the Net Promoter Score, a very simple, practical, operational, and reliable indicator which was designed to measure customer loyalty while overcoming the complexity of traditional customer surveys. As Reichheld observed, "most customer satisfaction surveys aren't very useful. They tend to be long and complicated, yielding low response rates and ambiguous implications that are difficult for operating managers to act on".[49] Reichheld's research, supported by Satmetrix, proved the link between higher Net Promoter Score and sustainable, profitable business growth. The approach inspired companies to move away from market research and instead focus on an operational, ongoing approach to customer experience.[50]

A Net Promoter Score is calculated using the answer to a single question, on a 0 – 10 scale: *'How likely is it that you would recommend [brand/product/service] to a friend or colleague?'* The responses are then grouped as follows:

> *Promoters* (score 9 – 10) are loyal enthusiasts who will keep buying and refer others.
> *Passives* (score 7 – 8) are satisfied but unenthusiastic customers who are vulnerable to competitive offerings.
> *Detractors* (score 0 – 6) are unhappy customers who can damage your brand and impede growth through negative word-of-mouth.

Subtracting the percentage of detractors from the percentage of pro-moters yields the Net Promoter Score, which can range from a low of -100 (if every customer is a detractor) to a high of 100 (if every customer is a promoter). The introduction of the Net Promoter Score has helped organisations to develop a more holistic understanding of the importance of the customer experience. The most successful implementations happen when the score becomes integrated into the business as a whole. It represents a philosophy of truly valuing customers as people. Whereas a purely accountancy-based approach leads businesses to chasing short term profits, the Net Promoter Score takes a long term view and focuses on the nurturing of loyal and passionate customers. It has an intrinsic ethical dimension, in that it helps to inspire companies to do the right things by its customers and employees, enriching their lives. As Rob Markey and Fred Reichheld note, the Net Promoter Score is "the business equivalent of the Golden Rule: Treat others as you would have them treat you".[51]

At the Sustainable Brands 2015 San Diego conference, John Schulz, AVP of Sustainability Operations at AT&T, discussed the way in which the Net Promoter Score was used to convince man-agement of the value in investing sustainability-related projects. According to Schulz, AT&T's Net Promoter Score doubled when customers became aware of their Corporate Social Responsibility programmes:

> The Net Promoter Score is elegant in its simplicity and its one question: *'Would you recommend AT&T products and services to a friend or colleague?'* This is a big deal at AT&T because while it is about customer support and satisfaction, it goes beyond that. We're asking customers if they are ac-tually going to tell their friends about this experience. So it's a powerful metric and one that means a lot to our business. We tried a couple of experiments. We used the power of the

simplicity of the metric and we took it to a couple of places. We looked at some of our key marketing programmes and we wanted to know what happens to our customers when they learn about the sustainability programmes we have in place. What effect does it have on their willingness to recommend us?

It Can Wait is our marketing programme to tell people about the dangers of distracted driving. We tested it before, telling customers about our programme; we tested it again, telling people about *Inspire*, our education programme, working to lower the high school dropout rate; and we also did a number of things where we looked at the Net Promoter Score across a pretty broad range of topics, including our environmental programmes like eco-rating, energy-efficiency programmes and water. What we found was kind of encouraging. When you think about this metric, of willingness to recommend, people get excited when it moves a tiny bit. The fact that you can show a doubling is impressive. When customers become aware of the kind of company we are, and where we want to go with this stuff, then they are more likely to recommend us. [52]

CEOs are now confirming that creating value for wider stakeholders helps profitability.[53] Given that customers, employees and other stakeholders increasingly care about what organisations stand for, businesses actively need to demonstrate their vision, purpose and values. This can only be done by building trust, something which can be done by better understanding stakeholders' views. Customer Experiences with Soul is not just a concept for commercial organisations though. As chapter three showed, the concept applies equally to individuals, government organisations, not-for-profit organisations and complex ecosystems of stakeholders. While it is not simple to achieve 100% coherence in a single organisation, the difficulty in creating a fully coherent organisational ecosystem which acts with a unified vision based on delivering extremely high levels of service, be they clients, customers or members of the public becomes even harder. But when driven by an authentic purpose and a desire to serve the public the results can be remarkable.

In 2004, the West Lothian Criminal Justice Project in Scotland was commissioned by the Lothian and Borders Criminal Justice Board to try to improve the summary justice system through a systems thinking methodology.[54] The systemic approach taken aimed to promote a different way of thinking about causes and effects; why the system was acting and performing in its current way. The project achieved dramatic results despite the huge complexity of the relationships within a legal system with so many different police, legal and political departments, authorities and parties involved. For example, end-to-end times from caution and charge to disposal were reduced from an average of 21 weeks to 8 weeks. Many other processes were redesigned, resulting in a significant impact on the efficiency, costs and use of resources. Not only were the quantitative results remarkable, staff throughout the system were also both positive and confident about the changes and did not want to return to the previous arrangements.

We define sustainability as the quality of our relationships. Our definition and approach to sustainability encourages business leaders to develop a more dynamic and systemic appreciation of all the relationships in both their business and environmental ecosystems, and how these interconnected relationships impact on their culture, mission and ultimately their bottom line. BrewDog is a good example of this principle in practice, being fanatical about reducing the distance between itself and its customers. James Watt describes BrewDog as being "a kind of modern day punk co-op that is ultimately about connectivity, culture and community".[55] They achieved this level of relationship and engagement with their customers through their groundbreaking Equity for Punks programme.

When BrewDog launched its first Equity for Punks fund-raising initiative in 2009, UK-based platforms such as Crowdcube, Seedrs and Banktothefuture which currently focus on equity-based crowd-funding were not in place. BrewDog had to look for potential part-ners to build a platform which would be technically capable for a project of this size and ambition. The first seven companies that BrewDog met to discuss this innovation all dismissed the idea as impossible. BrewDog did not give up but carried on until they found an eighth who thought the proposal "might just be possible". [56] In contrast to other crowdfunding platforms at the time which offered little security, BrewDog went through the full and formal approval regulation process leading to the creation of a bespoke system with the same standards as large-scale public listings.

The first Equity for Punks programme was launched in 2009 which not only saw £642,000 being raised with 1,300 people in-vesting; it also created, in BrewDog's words, a "legion of brand ambassadors around the globe". This was followed by Equity for Punks II which raised over £2.2m with an additional 5,000 new shareholders. In 2013, BrewDog broke all equity crowdfunding re-cords by raising £4.25m, which saw an additional 10,000 investors from 22 European countries.

BrewDog developed Equity for Punks because they wanted to put an end to the traditional, slightly adversarial paradigm, with pro-ducer and customer both playing a zero-sum game. They wanted to completely align their goals and objectives with those of the people who bought their beers, to lock their customers in for the long haul and ensure that the community as a whole all shared the same ob-jectives. This total belief in the power of authentic relationships with their best customers resulted in the fourth and most ambitious in-stalment of Equity for Punks, which raised £19.25m in the course of a year with 27,473 new investors joining. Equity for Punks IV broke the record in terms of the most money taken through crowdfunding of any business on record overall. It was also the first crowdfunding scheme to raise over £5m in under three weeks, and it was the first time that a company offered equity in tandem with bonds.[57]

Equity for Punks offers BrewDog and its investors much more than just a mechanism for investing in a company, with many equity punks investing mainly out of a shared desire to evolve craft beer and to be a part of the Equity Punks community which solidifies and nurtures the close relationship between BrewDog and the people who enjoy the beers they make. Watt describes Equity for Punks in the following manner:

> The Equity Punks community are the heart and soul of our business, and to have that community hyped about what we do has enabled us to grow as fast as we have over the last four years. We engage our equity punks in the decisions we make and how we grow, how we develop the business. They help us choose which beers to make, they help us to decide which cities to open bars in, and they are very much part of the team and part of the journey we are on as a company. So for us Equity for Punks has been really game changing.[58]

There are many benefits for those who purchase shares, such as discounts for their on-line shop and at BrewDog bars, exclusive access to new beers and invitations to the annual general meeting which is run more like a music festival. In April 2017 it was the most highly attended AGM in the UK, with 7,000 equity punks travelling to Aberdeen to take part. Equity for Punks IV closed in April 2016, resulting in a total of 42,316 BrewDog evangelists around the world. As Watt explains:

> Our shareholders are the absolute beating heart of our business. Launching Equity for Punks was the best decision we

ever made. We've turned more than 42,000 people into passionate brand ambassadors and raised enough money to keep the momentum of the craft uprising going in the process.[59]

The Equity Punks community have an exclusive BrewDog forum where they can discuss every aspect of BrewDog, its beers, its bars, its business, as well as having direct access to Watt and Martin Dickie (also a co-founder) in the 'Ask James and Martin' section. Not only does Watt regularly answer members' questions, the forum is BrewDog's richest source of feedback and new ideas. As Watt commented on the forum, "I love being involved in the discussions in here. A lot of our best ideas have came from discussions on these forums and it is great for me to know exactly what our most important people (our equity punks) are thinking!" And one equity punk made the comment to Watt, "One of the things that really impresses me about BrewDog is how active you are in here. I'm willing to bet not many companies have CEOs that talk to the shareholders on such a personal level, so kudos for that".

Founded in 1865 by shoemaker, William Timpson and his brother in law Walter Joyce, Timpson is a British retailer specialising in shoe repairs, key cutting & engraving, while offering additional services such as mobile phone repairs, jewellery and watch repair, and having 1550 outlets in the United Kingdom and Ireland. In terms of culture, attitude and history, it is a world apart from BrewDog. But when you explore its core philosophy, you discover that the management of Timpson focus on the very same two factors as BrewDog – offering a great product and investing in people. And just like BrewDog, those at the top of the company not only invest money in training programmes for their staff, but invest an extremely large percentage of their time continually developing and strengthening their personal relationships with every single member of staff in every single shop.

Timpson was started by the great great grandfather of chairman and chief executive John Timpson. His son James is the chief executive. Rather than staying in their head office, each week they relentlessly and single-mindedly visit their shops to see what is happening, aiming to visit each of the shops once a year. At the heart their philosophy lies the commonsense wisdom of giving those who actually know what they are doing the power to get on with it.[60] John Timpson sees much management theory as not being focused on results, but on doing things in the prescribed way, ticking the right boxes:

> If one day the business ended up in the hands of a professional management-school trained executive I think they could screw it up within twelve months. The reason is that they would squeeze the company in order to make easy profits. They would take all the power away from the people who actually serve the customers, they would look at the very significant support structure I've got in the field, they could chop that down, taking a million pounds out of the overheads, and put it straight into the bottom line for one year. I spend over three million in training. That could be cut. Probably two million saved there. And in the first year profit would soar. And within three years the business would have been completely screwed up.

The name he gives to his approach to business is 'upside-down management'.[61] Timpson believes his philosophy can work for anyone in any service organisation. At the heart lies one commonsense pearl of wisdom, that people in a service industry which does shoe repairs, watch repairs, cutting keys and engraving items need to be able to listen to customers and to be free to try and satisfy those wishes. It took John Timpson twenty years of being a chief executive to discover that the most important way to develop good customer service was simply to trust your people and to give them the freedom to get on with it and do it the way they think best:

It's obvious when you think about it, because really good customer service is dealing with the awkward problems, the difficult problems, the individual problems, and you can't give individual service through a set of rules. People can only deal with the difficult things and deal with the unexpected if they have got the freedom to do it their way.

Interestingly, when the company started to implement this management system in the late 1990s, because it was so different to what was the norm in most conventional organisations, branches, departments and production lines, Timpson recalls that "it was difficult to get people to believe what we actually said". It was quite a dramatic change of culture, especially since, historically many working in shoe repairs had an army background, responding to targets, rules, commands and a rigid structure. Not everyone in the company immediately bought in to the idea that you can offer great customer service by ensuring personal freedom. Some were uncomfortable working in a business which let them do what they wanted because they would have no one else to blame, and others were still unsure that it really was the case that they were authorised to decide how to resolve issues. The solution found to this dilemma was for each person to be told that they could spend up to £500 to settle a complaint without telling anyone else, and also that they could set their own prices. This was a significant freedom in a multi-branch organisation, but Timpson did it in order to demonstrate how strongly he felt that people needed to be set free.

It was not always plain sailing for the business. Not only did the new system fail to contribute to the bottom line straight away – it did not actually work. It took three years for people to realise that they would not get told off for breaking rules which did not exist, and that Timpson was serious. However, having taken time to settle in, the business now sees significant cost savings. Staff in the shops are able to settle complaints without the overheads associated with having a large customer care department, therefore making considerable cost savings. The introduction of upside-down management made the executive team pay more attention to individual employees, and the need for staff with the right personality.

This structure and way of working facilitates a very efficient form of organisational sensemaking and an effective way to listen to what staff have to say. Shop visits are not seen as a way to check up on people; their purpose is to find out where the good ideas are. Shop managers can experiment with ideas, and what works spreads to other shops. There is of course a middle layer in the organisation in the form of area managers, who Timpson describes as "the engine room of the organisation". They offer support to individual shops and administration, for example dealing with absence due to illness in shops which typically only have two or three people. This frees up the shops to focus on serving the customer. When going through the change from a command-and-control structure to an upside-down structure, the area managers had to learn not to issue orders, but how to support the people who worked for them. The business is an exceptional example of how purpose, methods, relationships, meaning and values all work together as a single whole to deliver a customer experience with soul, where there is full coherence across the whole organisation. As Timpson explains:

> We don't run the business. The business is run by people out there. We are simply there to support the people who are running the business. What works best actually is to genuinely, really want to be fantastic at looking after customers. Nothing would work unless the chairman and chief executive really believe in it. If you haven't got a passionate person running the business, who believes in it and wants to make it happen, it won't work.

In upside-down management we can see the same fundamental beliefs which we find in BrewDog's punk ethos:

> You've got to have the courage to ignore what other people
> do, and do it the way that you have discovered works. Then
> it becomes your business, doesn't it?

And the philosophy of Timpson is in total alignment with the trinity
at the centre of the holonomic circle:

> Every chief executive says that they value their people, but
> you have to do things which show people that you do actu-
> ally value them.

The hallmark of a strong and sustainable relationship is the ability
of two parties to achieve rapidly a shared understanding on a matter
which at first may seem ambiguous or which may not be fully understood. We can therefore see how the Equity Punks forum gives Watt
and members of the BrewDog team the ability to respond rapidly to
those people who they see as the most important in their ecosystem.
High quality networks are characterised by the quality of the flow
of communication and the ability to achieve a shared meaning. It is
'meaning' that we will now explore in the following section.

Meaning

The most powerful tool that a business leader has at their disposal is
thinking and the understanding of the relationship between thought,
language and experience. Just as it is important to exercise continually
to keep our bodies healthy, it is equally important to exercise our mental muscles, continually challenging ourselves to think and see in new
ways. Martial artists, sports people and musicians (to name just a few
disciplines) see no separation between mastery and practice. Practice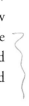
is not a sign of weakness and it is not a sign of not having achieved
mastery. There is a degree of self-awareness that allows athletes and

artists to continually monitor their actions and performance. In many corporate environments this sense of what mastery means is missing, and so the battles are ones of clashing egos rather than valiant efforts.

One key feature of thought is the way in which we use and apply metaphors, with one of the most dominant being that of seeing the organisation as a machine. In their book *The Systems View of Life: A Unifying Vision*, Fritjof Capra and Pier Luigi Luisi define life as having the following four major characteristics:[62]

1. Open Systems
    –   dissipative
    –   far from equilibrium
    –   continuous flow of energy and matter

2. The dynamics of flow as non-linear
    –   leads to the emergence of new levels of order

3. Self-generating networks
    –   networks where the boundary is distinct from the internal structure

4. Cognitive
    –   living systems interacting cognitively with the environment, in a way which is determined by its own internal organisation

When discussing organisational change, Capra sees that by and large the record of change management is poor. One of the main obstacles is our largely unconscious embrace of the metaphor of the machine. When implementing change management programmes, designs from outside are imposed through a mindset of top-down control, using machine-like language such as 're-engineering'. The problem with this metaphor is that machines do not change by

themselves (they are not living). The systems view of life sees human
organisations as having a dual nature – both living and non-living.
Organisations can be said to be alive in that they are communities of people with meaningful work. But organisations also have
a non-living aspect in that they are business entities with formal
structures.

In what way can human organisations be said to be alive? Capra
answers this question by saying that a human organisation is only
alive when it contains networks of communication. These informal
networks of communication are 'communities of practice':

> The aliveness of an organisation – its flexibility, creative
> potential, and learning capability – resides in its informal
> communities of practice.[63]

Organisations have both formal structures, such as sets of rules
which establish boundaries, and informal structures, which are fluid
and flowing networks of communication. There is a continual in-
terplay between formal structures and informal networks. A living
network responds to disturbances with structural changes and mes-
sages will be heard when they are meaningful:

> Living systems can only be disturbed. You give impulses
> rather than instructions.[64]

An example of these principles in practice is Spotify. Henrik Kniberg
is an agile coach who has spent much time working with Spotify, the
Swedish music streaming service which has 30 million users worldwide.[65] Kniberg describes Spotify's engineering culture as being characterised by its autonomous squads which are small, cross-functional,
self-organising teams, usually less than eight people in size. They sit
together and have end-to-end responsibility for the code they build.
Autonomy means responsibility for what to build, how to build it

and how to work together while doing it. The boundaries are the squad mission, product strategy and short term goals negotiated every quarter.[66]

Kniberg points out that the most valuable communication happens in informal and unpredictable ways. To support this Spotify also have tribes, chapters and guilds which are a "lightweight community of interest" where people across the whole company gather and share knowledge, such as leadership, web development or agile coaching. At Spotify the main focus is on community rather than hierarchical structure. Kniberg makes the observation that a strong community can get away with an informal, volatile structure and so Spotify can therefore be seen as being more alive than other more hierarchical and power-based organisations and businesses.

Interestingly, Kniberg likens the culture to a jazz band, where "each musician is autonomous and plays his own instrument, they listen and focus on the whole song together". He describes their culture as being one of high mutual respect, with colleagues often giving credit to each other for great work, and seldom taking credit for themselves. Spotify have managed to create a culture where the dysfunctional archetypes described in chapter three have been nurtured, with Kniberg observing that "considering how much talent we have here, there is surprisingly little ego".

So whether we are service designers, business leaders, team leaders or agile coaches, regardless of the methods we are working with, we continually have to communicate and nurture our purpose, developing high performance cultures which result in networks and ecosystems of high quality relationships where communication and meaning can flow freely. When we do, our organisations shift from being dead to alive, able to thrive and flourish. Behind all of these dimensions lie not just a belief in values, but really living your values each and every day, and so values make up the fifth principle of tools and techniques.

Values

Brian Goodwin, a revolutionary biologist and mathematician, always used to speak of how nature teaches us to do things with "minimum effort and maximum grace".[67] In organic living systems there is a dynamic relationship between the parts and the whole – maximum freedom of the parts and optimal coherence in the whole. This is the same as the philosophy of Chaordic, whose name was inspired by Dee Hock, the founder of VISA. Hock coined the term 'chaord' to describe the way in which living systems are creative, due to their existence at the 'edge of chaos' where both chaos and order coexist.[68] Leaders in a company must continually balance order and chaos, since too much control leads to an oppressive environment where creativity is stifled, but too much chaos on the other hand leads to collapse.

Chaordic were founded in 2010, and offer personalised e-commerce solutions to some of the largest retailers in Brazil, such as Saraiva and Nova Pontocom, whose brands include Casas Bahia, Ponto Frio and Extra. They have been recognised as the best company to work for in the state of Santa Catarina by Instituto Great Place to Work and Revista Amanhã. In September 2015, Chaordic joined forces with two other Brazilian technology companies, Linx S.A. and Neemu. While Chaordic have retained their name and identity, by coming under the umbrella of Linx they are now able to compete globally in offering a more fully integrated and comprehensive online multichannel shopping experience.

Simon came to know cofounder João Bernartt after being invited to run a two-day workshop for Chaordic on holonomic thinking. Chaordic is a young company, and so it is developing a Chaordic Academy to empower its staff and to develop holonomic approach to leadership. João explains it in this way:

> As we develop a clearer vision regarding the holonomic nature of doing business in this century, we will able to

this like *reads* *resurgitation*

combine the logical thinking and analysis required in the development of complex software, with sensing, feeling, intuition and emotions while dealing with people, developing products and experimenting with new business models.

really!

Chaordic truly are a business inspired by the dynamics of complex systems found in nature. João continues:

> Dee Hock's book *The Birth of the Chaordic Age* had a special influence on me, because I always believed in the complementarity of antagonistic characteristics such as chaos and order. At the time of reading the book I was trying to better understand the characteristics that led to major technological innovations. I realised that the main innovations came from emergence, and not by force or imposition on people through command and control structures.

Chaordic have at their heart a simple set of principles, captured by the acronym AC-DC which in Portuguese are the first letters of 'love', 'consciousness', 'discipline' and 'commitment'. As we saw with BrewDog's charter, creating a set of principles is only the first step in living and leading with them:

> Having a clear purpose and principles already set us apart from a lot of companies. It is very easy to write a list of principles. But being faithful to them, and living them to their full requires a lifetime of dedication. There are very few companies who are able to walk this path in life.

João is an engineer who studied in both Brazil and in France. While studying for his masters degree in artificial intelligence in 2006 he was looking for some books on Amazon, and was impressed by how they were able to change the site dynamically, showing him more products which were related to his tastes:

> This impressed me at the time and I thought that I could do this kind of thing here in Brazil. None of the websites in Brazil had this kind of feature at the time and I started to think that if I could build a product and deliver to all the e-commerce companies in Brazil, I could have a good product.

João started to study collaborative filtering and data mining, and by coincidence Netflix launched a competition to see which coders and developers could build a recommendation system 10% faster than their own. João and two friends formed a team and managed to build a system which was 6.7% faster and which came second in the competition. Realising that they had developed something which could be turned into a commercially viable product, the team started to search for funding, and with the help of a government grant Chaordic was born in 2009. João recalls their inspirations for the way in which Chaordic would be modelled:

> We started to study the companies we admired. We read a lot about Pixar, Apple, Amazon, Google – there were many.  We saw that every company which was making a difference had a clear purpose which drove the entire focus of the company. When we read the book by Dee Hock we studied a lot about chaordic systems and chaordic organisations. Hock also said you must have a purpose.
>
> In order to be able to work in a harmonious way, every group of people must have a common purpose. Everybody has an intrinsic purpose – your unique personality. I really like to study companies – how to create politics, structures, systems

which create a company – and this has allowed me to form my particular way of seeing a company. Lots of people in Chaordic love to program. This is their unique purpose, what they intrinsically want to do inside Chaordic. These guys, who are software programmers, and I must have a common purpose between us. What is our common purpose? To personalise the world.

Once you have understood your purpose, the next thing to understand is how your purpose is going to be achieved. A purpose can be realised in many different ways, and so principles are required which will tell you if you have reached your goal.

The word 'principles' is interesting for João, who sees it in three different ways:

The first way of understanding 'principles' is as the beginning of something. You can say "Ah, it's the principle of the universe". Every beginning of something is a principle. So we can use the concept of 'principle' as the beginning of something.

Another way to define 'principle' for us is in relation to the laws of nature, mainly the physical laws. Everything which explains how the physical world works, mainly in physics. When you study physics you study a lot of principles.

The third way in which people use the term 'principles' is in relation to moral laws. When you say "he is a very principled person" you are talking about the laws of morality and altruism. We believe that when you are acting from these kind of laws you can achieve success and happiness. It is important for every company, every person and every group of people to establish a set of principles.

We asked João if he could explain in more detail why Chaordic's AC-DC principles (in Portuguese *amor, consciência, disciplina,* and *compromisso*) were chosen:

> The first principle is *love*. Love for us is very important. It's not just about loving what you do but also what you offer society, and what the company is offering society. This first principle is the most important of all. When you act in your company in any way with love, you can do everything better, and you can cope better with difficulties.

> The second principle is *consciousness*. The exact definition of consciousness is not simple, and for us, the definition is 'the search for the truth'. For us, it is extremely difficult to discover exactly what truth is, but searching for the real meaning in something – the truth – this means looking for consciousness.

> The third principle is *discipline,* which we define as every-thing that you don't like. Love provides an equilibrium between the principles. Love is about what you like to do, such as loving work and also loving things outside of work, including what you are doing for others. By contrast, disci-pline is what you don't like to do. For example, nobody says you have to have discipline when eating ice-cream, because everybody likes eating ice-cream. But you need discipline to wake up very early in the morning since it is not very nice to wake up very early. There are many times when both companies and people have to learn rapidly, and to change and adapt quickly – actions which are intrinsically related to

nonsense

discipline, because discipline makes you learn fast, it makes you change fast and adapt fast. Discipline lies at the root of the reasons for rapid change.

The final principle is an interchangeable principle, meaning that it is the only one which can be used at times one way, and at other times another. The last 'C' of AC-DC could be *commitment*, and we have previously used 'courage' (*coragem*) and 'knowledge' (*conhecimento*) for example, but on the whole we use 'commitment'. Commitment lies beyond discipline and so is extremely important when you really want to do something because you really need commitment to get there. It's an intrinsic feeling, an emotion that makes you go straight ahead while overcoming obstacles to reach your goal.

For us, these four principles were the answers for how we would like to achieve our purpose. At Chaordic we will not change our principles very frequently. They are something that we believe will still be the same two hundred years from now. Having defined our principles we were then able to write our values. Our values can change year by year because they depend on the conditions of the company – what the next challenge is which we need to overcome. They are more flexible.

Chaordic are still relatively young, both in the age of the company and the average age of people who work there, with many of their team falling into the millennial demographic. It is interesting to see that despite this generation of entrepreneurs and coders having an underlying sense of a new way of working together, the company still works hard on expressing, articulating and reaching a joint understanding of their values, as do BrewDog. Hence 'meaning' and 'values' are inherently interlinked.

The five universal human values of peace, truth, love, righteousness and non-violence form one of the key pillars of *Holonomics*. When these human values are in place, there is much less reliance on rules, bureaucracy and control, allowing organisations become agile, resilient and sustainable, being better able to evolve as changes in the environment demand. No matter what life may throw at us, with human values operating we are all able to align ourselves behind a single vision; we are valued as human beings, and solutions can emerge naturally, as and when they are needed. These universal human values are the foundation of authenticity, agility and change and relate to our understanding of humanity and what it means to be human. For this reason, the holonomic circle does not include the single word 'values' as organisations more commonly understand the term; it has the more profound universal term 'human values', which we will now explore in greater detail.

5. The Holonomic Circle: Human Values

Education in Human Values

According to the Indian programme *Education in Human Values* created by educator Sathya Sai Baba, the great aim of education is the development of character. At the heart of the programme are the five universal human values of peace, truth, love, righteousness and non-violence, which are developed from inside of the students. These five human values are very powerful, because they focus on relationships. They form the ethical and spiritual foundation of an organisation, allowing people to connect, communicate and work together in teams in order to achieve common goals. Authentic dialogue becomes possible, allowing people to overcome seemingly intractable problems.

Maria is a leading business strategist in Brazil, having worked closely with Robert Kaplan and David Norton, introducing and developing their Balanced Scorecard methodology in many of the largest national and multinational corporations in Brazil and Latin America, covering a wide range of sectors including telecoms, technology, petrochemicals, steel, energy, transportation and education. She started her career first as an analyst in corporate finance and then moved into private banking, where she provided financial advice for high net worth individuals and families.

Maria studied economics at the University of Campinas (Unicamp), driven by her deep desire to really understand how the world of economics actually worked. She is also an educator, a lifetime vocation, and was involved in the development of the Brazilian movement *Todos Pela Educação* (Education for All) which has the objective of ensuring a high quality of public education for all children by the year 2022. From quite a young age Maria's curiosity also embraced the study of eastern religions and scriptures, leading her to visit India in 2009. In 2012 she became a qualified instructor in the *Education in Human Values* programme.

Although the programme is aimed at school teachers, it became clear to Maria that *Education in Human Values* could also be applied in a corporate and business environment, and so for the last few years she has been discussing the universal human values with CEOs, presidents, executives and entrepreneurs across many different industries, sectors, sizes and countries. Her approach has been to introduce human values into leadership, business strategy and change management programmes, developing a way to facilitate dialogue and deep discussions about why processes, methodologies and frameworks fail to produce the expected results and outcomes following their implementation.

In an organisation everything is perceived as separate; for example, you have many separate concepts – strategy, execution, production, marketing, operations etc. There are many companies where the vision is not common and not shared between everyone, and neither is the strategy. Developing a corporate strategy must involve helping everyone in the whole organisation to think more deeply about what is the essence of the strategy and what lies behind the development of a strategy. If it is just a hidden agenda about making more money, if it is not authentic and the purpose is not legitimate, then people will not be engaged. Many problems are caused by a lack of authenticity, a lack of clear purpose, and the lack of seeing everyone in the same whole, with everyone feeling a part of the whole.

One of the teachings of *Education in Human Values* is the analogy of the ocean – what happens at the surface and what it is like below. At the depths of the ocean all is tranquil and calm, but as a result of the wind, temperature, pressure and many other factors, the surface can be agitated, choppy and at times turbulent. This analogy teaches us that we are all the same in our essence, but on the surface we are different as we all have different experiences in life, we live in different circumstances and we have different levels of education, and so on.

If we only relate to what we see on the surface, we end up acting in opposition to the five human values, judging people superficially, ending up with conflicts, arguments, unethical behaviour. The surface values act like personal values, for example, valuing aggression, conflict, dominance, arrogance, theft, abuse of power, violence, deceit, status and status symbols. The result is instability, confusion, unhappiness, dissatisfaction and inequality. The human values lie in the depth of the ocean, enabling us to develop a level of consciousness which allows us to understand that while others are different on the surface, we all share the same essence. When we connect with people, no matter who they may be or how they are acting, we have an ability to connect with their essence. This is a meeting of two essences, which are in fact one. People will bring things which are different from ourselves, because on the surface we are different. With the five human values operating at the deep level, it is important to have tolerance, because there are any number of factors relating to a person's past or current challenges which lead them to act out of ego and fear, displaying dysfunctional archetypal behaviours.

Living the human values allows us to more fully understand the underlying reasons for someone's behaviour and why that person is acting in any particular way. When you live the human values, you can see more about a situation. If someone manifests behaviour in a way which we do not expect and our lives do not have the grounding which the human values provide, we do not know what to do or how to respond. This also applies to cross-generational situations. In organisations nowadays where things are changing a lot, it is vital to have a certain form of stability, otherwise people will become lost. When human values are present, they provide this stability, so that those who are from Generation X or the Baby Boom generation know how to interact with Generation Y, Millennials and other groups with norms which are different from them. Change is not a problem, because it is natural to have difference and creativity, and innovation no longer becomes forced or imposed.

The human values also apply at the organisational level, and how people in an organisation act as a whole. If these people just stay on the surface they will just create conflict, and they will try to sell more in an artificial way. At best this results in the creation of an artificial image of your brand in order to please everybody. However, what can happen are scandals such Wells Fargo, which came to light in September 2016. Employees of the bank signed up customers for current accounts and credit cards without their knowledge, and created around two million fake accounts with forged signatures, email addresses, and fake PIN numbers, all as a result of pressure from senior management. Many of the bank's victims did not realise they had been signed up for these fake banking products, and their credit ratings were adversely affected for not keeping up to date the accounts which they did not even know about.[69]

The five universal human values have been discussed for several thousand years and can be found in the ancient writings scripture of masters, sages and holy people. The values are universal, since their role is to help humanity to evolve and to guide people towards a better experience of life. When we live our lives without human values we become disconnected from everything, and this is due to ignorance, because we have forgotten who we are and why we are here. We do not explore these deeper issues of who we are. Because humanity did not progress and develop, this separation and experience of fragmentation have become bigger and bigger. This has led to us having a sense of separation on many levels – poor and rich, between countries, between colleagues and people in other social groups, between ourselves and nature – there are many ways to experience separation and fragmentation. We are living in a special moment where we are now reconnecting. It is as if the issues that we now all face together as humanity are like portals, opening up to allow us to redefine and reconnect. So we are seeing people rediscovering their relationship with nature, working to restore rivers, to save and protect animals, as well as reconnecting more with people, which includes connecting via the internet and social technology.

Our current situation is paradoxical – people have both the desire to reconnect and the technology available to do so, but since we still have a mentality of separation, the result can be one of confusion. The universal human values are the essence of connecting and relating to others, and so this is why we promote the discussion of them and how to reintroduce them into business and society, thus guiding people out of this confusion and resolving the paradox.

The five universal human values of peace, truth, love, righteousness and non-violence are presented in Figure 5, along with many of their sub-values.[70] These sub-values help to explain what each universal human value means in practice. The values should not be approached in a fragmented manner. When explaining and discussing one particular value or sub-value, it is possible to see that all of the others are also present. Each value has an identity and yet does not have an identity, there being a dynamic relationship between the whole and the parts.

Peace	Truth	Love	Righteousness	Non-violence
Self-respect	Honesty	Sharing	Trust	Toleration
Self-confidence	Integrity	Caring	Resourceful	Concern for
Reflection	Truthfulness	Sympathy	Duty	all life
Perseverance	Awareness	Devotion	Self-reliance	Selfless service
Inner silence	Wisdom	Dedication	Determination	Sacrifice
Patience	Understanding	Compassion	Usage of time	Self-satisfaction
Optimism	Sincerity	Kindness	Responsibility	Respect
Humility	Spirit of	Forgiveness	Usage of	Harmony
Observing	Inquiry	Friendship	resources	Citizenship
Faith	Reasoning	Gratitude	Morality	Global
Calm	Intuition	Empathy	Initiative	awareness
Concentration	Knowledge	Appreciation	Higher goals	Fellow feeling
Fortitude	Focus	Equality	Right company	Brotherhood
Maintaining	Discrimination	Generosity	Discipline	Appreciation
equanimity	Quest for	Charity	Dedication	Fearlessness
Dignity	Knowledge	Happiness	Reliability	Courage
Being	Curiosity	Unity	Good	Self-control
contented	Creativity	Loyalty	character	Helpfulness
Balance	Simplicity		Good manners	Justice
Loyalty			Conscience	Ethics
Forbearance			Consideration	
			Cooperation	
			Cleanliness	
			Simple living	
			Leadership	

Figure 5: Human Values and their Sub-Values

The best way to introduce the human values into organisations is through dialogue. We do not introduce the values in a stand-alone fashion; we integrate and promote them during discussions on high performance, change programmes, strategy workshops and of course in relation to customer experience. We now provide examples which can be used as templates to inspire discussions in your own places of work.

Peace

If a company commits to working with the five universal human values, nominating them as the values they will implement, then they will not have problems such as understanding their client. Peace as a core value allows people to listen and to be more mindful of their interactions no matter who they are interacting with. Intel's code of conduct is divided into six sections – Customer Orientation, Discipline, Quality, Risk Taking, Great Place to Work and Results Orientation.[71] Listening is listed as the first value under the first section, Customer Orientation:

> We strive to:
> Listen and respond to our customers, suppliers and stakeholders.
> Clearly communicate mutual intentions and expectations.
> Deliver innovative and competitive products and services.
> Make it easy to work with us.
> Excel at customer satisfaction.

While discussing values at a conference in São Paulo in 2016, we met an analyst from Intel, and it was interesting for us to see that Intel ID cards are always worn with an additional card with Intel's values. Intel's customer experience is not just about the way in which people interact with their products and services; it also refers to the way in which people do business with them and how people work with them. This emphasises the point that you cannot design the customer experience because you *are* the customer experience.

Related to 'listening' is the need for respect for others. 'Self-respect', 'self-confidence' and 'inner silence' are all together under 'peace' because you can only be at peace if you have peace within yourself, if you have self-confidence and if you have self-respect. Before you can respect another person you have to be able to respect yourself.

Part of our work involves coaching senior executives and the members of their teams, which requires strong listening skills and asking people how they are really feeling about their work. Maria recalls a conversation she had in one company where a member of a team felt that a great injustice had been done:

> This person told me that they were feeling injustice and I asked why? When you explore the circumstances in depth to more fully understand, you often discover that the sense of injustice comes from inside the person and not the situation itself. This case was interesting because the person told me that they were in a position lower than they felt that they should have been, because they were delivering what the company was asking them to do. In addition, the company was contracting people from outside in higher positions to those in his team and department. They said to me that they were doing a lot and that internal clients recognised the quality of their work, and so they felt that they were ready to be promoted to a higher position.

> I talked to their manager about this. The company had in fact offered a vacancy to them in a more senior position but they had not accepted, saying that they were not yet ready or prepared for it. It was a surprise to me to hear their comment that opportunities were not open to them, so I asked them to explain a little more. What soon became clear was that it was a lack of self-confidence and fear which had created this contradictory situation for them.

Companies need to develop self-confidence in people across the whole organisation, and not only in those who they identify as leaders or who have leadership potential. Having observed that what often happens in many companies is to the contrary, Maria coined the phrase 'as empresas são muito generosas nas cobranças e muito parcimoniosas nas celebrações' which means 'companies are generous in their accusations but miserly in their praise'. Many companies have cultures in which individuals are criticised more than they are praised, because if they celebrate something which that individual did well, other people fear that two things may happen. The first is that they believe that the individual may end up thinking that they have nothing else to learn, that they are the best. And secondly, that the individual will ask to be promoted. So companies do not celebrate things, always taking the position that employees have more to learn. When giving feedback, more time is spent telling people what they lack rather than seeing the situation more positively, for example, recognising an individual's underlying competence, and so looking to see how they can develop and gain knowledge and new skills.

Such situations rob people of their self-confidence. There are many with very 'crazy' and unsettling working environments in which many leaders believe that their position means that they have to be seen to be the best, closing their ears to any criticism, due to a false belief that they do not have anything else to learn. These leaders feel that they have to demonstrate and project a very high level of self-confidence. Even during times when they lack confidence they still have to pretend otherwise. An unintended consequence for those in subordinate positions below is that the leaders create a culture in which people do not believe in themselves.

If someone is not at peace within themselves they are not able to listen and have constructive and enjoyable conversations. In meetings in business cultures which are based on status, if someone makes a comment or suggestion then other people often feel that they have to respond in a way which shows that they have power, perhaps by criticising or subtly putting that person down, diminishing their value. These types of relationship are created through a lack of self-confidence and peace, and they create very toxic environments without soul. People behave more like actors and end up further and further away from their authentic selves.

The human values are of direct relevance to innovation, with toxic environments stifling creativity, confidence and authentic dialogue. Patience is also a sub-value of 'peace', and this applies to innovation, because it relates to the timing of actions, and to understanding when the right time is for something to flourish and come to fruition. Jack Dorsey is one of the creators and founders of Twitter, having had the idea for the service in 2001. However, the technology was not then available, and it was not until 2006 that the company was founded and his vision became a reality. When he came to Brazil in 2014, he made the point that as an entrepreneur you have to show your ideas to people and positively welcome feedback.[72] Not only do you have to be able to recognise when someone else is wrong; you also have to have the courage to recognise that other people's feedback, however harsh, may be right. But just as he had the idea for Twitter many years before web technology allowed his idea to become viable, there are times when you have to have the patience to park an idea and then come back to it later when the conditions are ready for it to both function and flourish.

The story of Twitter is an interesting case in which both values and a subsequent lack of those values played out, first as Twitter was developed and launched, becoming one of the world's most popular social networks, and secondly in the disputes which then followed between the founders, with some feeling that their role in the success was never fully acknowledged by others. As we saw from João's comments in the previous chapter, a company must work continually on its values and must never be complacent, allowing its culture to degrade.

Truth

Truth is the most difficult value to understand. We have the idea that truth is something related to our mind. So, for example, we all have our own truth based on things that we believe, but from the perspective of the universal human values 'truth' refers to those things which do not change. Intuition is related to truth, because intuition is that inner voice telling us something which did not pass through our minds. It is that truth inside yourself which is there, but to which we do not listen because of the emotional layers affecting our cognition.

'Curiosity' is closely related to 'intuition'. Sathya Sai Baba, the Indian educator who created Education in Human Values, always said that before you decide to follow a teacher, religion or guru you have to observe their actions and ask many questions, and if the answers that you receive really resonate with you, then that is your path. The fact that he talked about the need to question without blindly accepting someone else's truth is important, because curiosity provides us with an ability to see that we are not happy with the answers given, or what is really happening, for example in a situation at work. It inspires us to look deeper, revealing more layers and dimensions of a phenomenon that we might have otherwise missed.

Much of *Holonomics* was written to help people to better explore the manner in which they think, how they construct reality, and the way in which we are able to receive and understand some aspect of the truth of a situation without this concept being the actual or whole truth. Hence we introduced Henri Bortoft's distinction between 'dogmatic annunciations' and 'constructive conceptions'.[73] While many people like to refer to paradigms and the need to change our own, genuine shifts in paradigm are very rare. We can become trapped into thinking that our current mode of cognition and our understanding of reality is the right way and the only way, a stance which prevents many people from being able to make a genuine leap from an old paradigm into a new one.

Thomas Kuhn argued that the prevailing activity of science takes place during long periods of 'normal science'.[74] This normal science gives way to a 'scientific revolution' in which theories and ideas change in radical ways as whole new systems of concepts are created. These overall systems of concepts are called paradigms. Building on Kuhn's theory of the structure of scientific revolutions, David Bohm and F. David Peat argued that during periods of normal science quite significant changes do in fact take place. True creativity, they argued, cannot be bounded to periods of scientific revolution alone.[75] For Bohm and Peat, new ideas arise due to changes in metaphor. Metaphoric perception is therefore fundamental to all science, and it involves bringing together previously incompatible ideas in radically new ways. If we can understand the metaphors by which we live we can better understand how we are constructing reality, and therefore what we accept as truth.

'The Deep Science Walk' is an experiential learning concept that we created and which weaves together those elements relating to the history of science which run throughout *Holonomics,* structured to imbue within people a deeply intuitive sense of what a paradigm shift really entails, and how they too can develop 'metaphoric perception' and creative insights. The experience is one of authentic co-creation. Science is not taught as dogma; rather, participants are encouraged to explore together the underlying meaning of the topics introduced.

The Deep Science Walk takes participants through the history of science, starting with the Ancient Greeks. Participants are introduced to one particular era in the history of science, with a brief presentation of the ideas of two or three philosophers or scientific discoveries from that period. Participants break into groups of two or three people to discuss their impressions of this particular era, and then report back to the group as a whole. We then provide our own observations, and we discuss additional philosophers, scientists and theories.

For each era, a number of printed pictures are handed out representing those scientists, the philosophies and the scientific theories. Participants place these on the walls of the room, thus building up a graphical representation of this history of science, including the respective dates. The Deep Science Walk ends with the room containing a full circle of pictures, all with the respective dates which the participants are then able to wander around, contemplating the whole of the history of science in a single visual representation which also represents leaps of creative insight, paradigm shifts and changes in world views. It is a provocative and powerful experience.

The participants taking part are given space to contemplate how their own mental models and metaphors currently impact on their own world views, and how new creative insights could be gained. They are also able to develop insights in relation to how other people construct reality, and learn to better empathise with those who have different world views and life experiences from their own. By inserting exercises, such as playing with prisms (an exercise we describe in detail in *Holonomics*), they have an opportunity to contemplate the differences between Newton and Goethe and therefore begin to understand how they can expand their awareness from thinking into to the four ways of knowing the world, as explained in chapter three.[76] This expansion and transition of consciousness enables creative insights, resulting in radically new ways of comprehending nature, the universe and reality.

Love

At times we sometimes create an artificial division between what happens inside the company, for example production, marketing, selling – activities which we sometimes perceive as contrary to our values and how we are as people outside the company. There are times when people in an organisation strive to evolve more conscious ways of working and introducing self-organisation for example, but who nonetheless feel guilty when taking part in activities which are deemed by some to be of a 'lower' level of consciousness, such as taking time out for personal self-development. One of the dangers of codified hierarchical models of consciousness is that people will interpret them in many different ways, with an ironic side-effect that instead of becoming authentically whole, an implicit form of elitism is engendered and false sense of superiority is felt from a 'higher-level' perspective of reality. It is very easy to 'understand' a hierarchical model intellectually, but it is far more difficult to fully absorb and live by the behaviours and wisdom described in the 'higher' levels, especially if we have hidden archetypes operating within us which blind us to the negative and harmful aspects of ourselves.

The holonomic circle was created to promote a dialectical approach to the exploration of customer experiences with soul, and therefore rather than taking an approach in which consciousness is modelled hierarchically, it is founded on the phenomenological discovery that our experience of reality is already whole, and that each element of the circle encountered in the expression of the others. This is particularly true of love, in that when we are fully acting out of love, the dangers of falling into an elitist conception of consciousness is greatly reduced due to connecting with people at the level of their essence.

Kyocera's corporate motto is holonomic: "Respect the divine and love people".[77] As we saw in the previous chapter, Chaordic's values start with love, but it is still quite rare to find the mention of love in a corporate vision. But it is possible to bring these values associated with love into companies – values such as happiness, devotion and sharing. Loyalty is an important sub-value, because businesses desire loyal customers and as a result there are many different loyalty programmes in existence. But what lies at the heart of these? Is the essence only a desire to sell more, or is it more a case that selling more the result of having really loyal clients?

A customer experience with soul is a sacred experience. Within love we find sub-values such as sympathy, dedication, compassion and gratitude. We are grateful when someone buys our product and becomes loyal to our business. Maria began her career in private banking, which is very intimate and can often involve considerable psychology. In this type of activity a person has to be able to develop very trusting relationships; these are what are valuable, and so care has to be taken with this type of relationship, because a service is being sold to the client. This involves being grateful to the client, caring for them, sharing with them, and having love for them.

Righteousness

Within 'righteousness', one sub-value which really stands out is 'usage of resources'. If resources are used inefficiently, the result is unnecessary waste, so sustainability is inherently related to righteousness, as it is to all of the values.

In righteousness we also find 'dedication'. Righteousness therefore relates directly to leadership, teamwork and high performance cultures. When we work in a company we have specific responsibilities for certain things. Sometimes people do not commit the effort which their work deserves. Work is sacred, in that it can be seen as a sacred act. Any act of work becomes a sacred moment when you are putting your best into that action. It is the opportunity to put into practice the best of you, for example good character, good manners, conscience – all values which we find associated with righteousness.

One part of the programme within *Education for Human Values* looks at ways in which we can limit our personal desires for consumption. When we are full of such desires, we lose both our humanity and the best way to do things. The sub-value 'usage of time' falls under righteousness, because when we waste our time we are not doing things which contribute to the good of both people and planet. If you want to have a high-performance culture in a company, you have to have righteousness. This means thinking about values such as our use of time, dedication, self-reliance, initiative, cooperation and morality. Having a culture where there is morality means being able to follow rules and really being fully conscious about the community of which you are a part. These are not bureaucratic rules but the societal agreements that we have in order to be able to live together. If we do not follow these and fail to respect other people, we will not have righteousness and we will therefore not be able create an environment which enables individuals to develop new ideas and to innovate, and be able to relate to clients and customers.

Non-violence

Non-violence does not just refer to physical violence. Any act can be an act of violence if there is not a suitable level of awareness, attention and respect for other people. In this value we find 'tolerance' which is essential for good work environments, especially as it helps us to respect and understand diversity in organisations. 'Self-satisfaction' is also in non-violence, but this does not mean being big-headed or full of ourselves; it means knowing what we want in life and knowing that we do not desire more than we need. It means being satisfied with our life. If we do not feel this satisfaction we ought to become motivated to work and change our approach in order to improve. So we must understand ourselves in relation to satisfaction. If we are not self-satisfied, it becomes more probable that we will carry out an act of violence.

In Britain many forms of corruption exist at the highest levels of society, but it is often well hidden, for example, in off-shore business deals which very rarely become public. In Brazil people have to deal with the daily realities of corruption, not just that which is reported in the news, but which happens at every level of society, with those in positions of power taking money from the health system, from hospitals, schools – money which would have been spent curing people and feeding children, for example. People who are corrupt are very poor inside themselves and full of negative attitudes. It can feel particularly shocking when very wealthy and privileged people are seen to be acting in a corrupt manner. These are people with very special, indeed remarkable, positions in society. It is often the case that there is a lack of love and also so many negative emotions inside themselves that they compensate by obsessively obtaining more and more. If a person does not resolve all their other issues, for them nothing will ever be enough.

It is interesting to contemplate a value such as 'citizenship', since this refers to relationships between all the stakeholders in a business ecosystem. At times it can seem that organisations and businesses see themselves as separate from communities, missing the systemic aspects of being a part of a greater whole. When we implement the five universal human values, awareness about citizenship is developed, and thinking about what we have to do to help the community comes naturally. A sense of community does not just refer to the external relations between an organisation and its stakeholders. A sense of community can also be nurtured inside an organisation as a part of its culture. This sense of culture cannot be nurtured and encouraged where the leaders do not have courage and fearlessness. Discernment rather than judgement is vital in knowing how to respond and deal with people inside organisations who are weak, and who at times find themselves in difficult or threatening positions. These people will often respond not by taking personal responsibility, but by claiming that it is always others who are to blame, and not themselves. Manipulating people into thinking that others are to blame and cynically and subtly allowing people to form a negative image of others are forms of violence, because it involves accusing people of getting something wrong and therefore creating a general perception that other people are in some way bad or less able than is the actual case.

Cognitive dissonance is the psychological phenomenon experienced as mental stress which comes about when we attempt to hold contradictory beliefs and attitudes held simultaneously. Rather than exploring the contradiction in a rational and calm manner, quite often we act in an emotional manner to reduce the dissonance, and this can happen by simply rejecting new information which contradicts our existing beliefs. Cognitive dissonance can apply to the way in which we think about others. Individuals who are in powerful positions of high status are able to manipulate people and situations with little risk of others changing their beliefs about who they are, their reputations, motives and values.

The danger for leaders is not being able to recognise acts of violence which may be happening but which may be going undetected. The consequence for a company of not being able to resolve these issues internally can be an exodus of staff, many leaving a company because of this type of personality in a leadership position. This form of violence can often be quite subtle and hard for others to detect. A business may have people who are doing good jobs and are outwardly happy, but when the leaders lack courage and have feelings of feel fear, this can result in the business losing high-quality employees. These factors are all related to non-violence.

When you live the human values you do not have to artificially create customer experiences. The ability to develop customer experiences with soul means having the ability to relate from within, a 'within' which must be in harmony with the essence of the company. If not, there will be incoherence between how you express your self, what you mean, and how you act and interact with those around you.

The essence of the universal human values can be summarised with the following guidance:

- You have to be in peace with yourself.
- Your thoughts, speech and actions must all be in alignment, and for this to happen you have to be committed to the truth. Truth is essential in order for clients and customers to have a good relationship with a brand and an organisation, because if you cannot deliver

something, it is always better to be truthful rather than dishonest.

⬇ You must have unconditional love for everyone and everything.

⬇ You have to act correctly in order to be reliable and transparent.

⬇ You have to be non-violent, which means really listening to others and having authentic dialogue in order to be able to explore new ways of seeing.

When the five universal human values are present in an organisation, relationships between customers and brands become more solid, wisdom is developed, people are able to make better choices, and lives become happier. Human values improve relationships between each individual in an organisation, team, network or ecosystem, but it is not the case of simply introducing the concept once. It is a continual learning process where everyone is learning, and not just some. This means that leaders must stimulate the spirit of learning within teams, with clients, partners along the value chain, and principally, with themselves.

The next chapter further develops our understanding of the customer experience, searching for an answer as to what exactly something *is,* and learning which questions we need to ask in order to understand *being.* We will move away from exploring tools and techniques which are involved in designing customer experiences with soul, and shift our focus onto the very essence of *experience.*

6. The Holonomic Circle –
The Transcendentals

The Elements of Being

Hans-Georg Gadamer was a German philosopher born on 11th February 1900, best known for his seminal work *Truth and Method*, a treatise on philosophical hermeneutics which was first published in 1960. The Greek term *hermenia* referred to translation and interpretation and related to the challenges that early Christian philosophers such as Augustine (354–430) had in relation to translating Greek thought into the Christian message, and the need to translate Scripture into conceptual terms. Not only was Gadamer one of the world's greatest philosophers on hermeneutics, he was also a great student of the philosophy of Plato (c. 424–348/347 BC), starting his studies at the age of twenty under the guidance of the great scholar and thinker Paul Natorp (1854–1924), who suggested that Gadamer write his doctoral dissertation on pleasure in the Platonic dialogues.[78] To aid him in his studies, Gadamer would study with Martin Heidegger (1889–1976), the philosopher who published the astounding work *Being and Time* in 1927, and who at the time was the assistant to Edmund Husserl (1859–1938), the founder of the philosophical movement of phenomenology.

Before Plato, society struggled to understand the notion of abstract and conceptual thought. Even the great mathematician Theaetetus (417–369 BC) was susceptible to confusing the constantly changing physical components of the sensory world, the ideal components of a classification system, and the abstract notion of mathematics itself.[79] In this ancient epoch people had not yet been able to understand that it was possible to come up with a mathematical proof that the angles in a triangle always add up to 180 degrees, as opposed to always needing to measure the angles empirically.

In his writings Plato posited a *chorismos* – a two-world system. Gadamer did not interpret the *chorismos* as an ontological separation, i.e. the literal existence of two independent worlds or universes.[80] He took the view that Plato had to posit this separation to help us to understand the methodological differences between that which we can experience though our senses, and 'ideal realities' such as abstract thinking and the basic elements of mathematics.[81] Gadamer came to the conclusion that the major concern for Plato was in understanding the nature of the One and the many (or in modern language the whole and the parts). So what we discover in Gadamer's writings on Plato is a wide-raging doctrine as to how humans can live together, based on the recognition that we live our lives in a web of meaning.

Gadamer lived to be 102 years old. His lifetime study of Plato began with the publication of his university thesis in 1922, and ended with his last published work in 1991, a span of seventy years. Henri Bortoft met Gadamer when he was 86, and one observation Henri made was that while many philosophers at conferences would turn up, present their papers and then leave, Gadamer was authentic, "the real deal", staying for the whole conference, listening intently. Even when others disagreed with him, rather than arguing he would make every effort to help those who did disagree to articulate their thoughts more clearly, wishing to help them to understand better the points that they were trying to make.

Gadamer wrote that "to be in a conversation means to be beyond oneself, to think with the other, and to come back to oneself as if another".[82] Conversation was central to the life of Gadamer, as we can see in his studies of Plato and Socrates, themselves two of the greatest practitioners of dialogue.[83] In Plato and Socrates we see the desire to help strengthen the arguments of others, always trying to see a situation or an idea from the point of view of the other, and Gadamer carried on this tradition when interacting and conversing with people.

Hermeneutics is less a written structured methodology, and more a way of approaching the study of a text or a work of art as a conversation. Within the process of having this conversation one's own self-understanding is restructured. Gadamer always emphasised that, especially in relation to written works, we should always attempt to take the other in their intention and not in their expression. This is by no means easy of course, since the majority of time we do not have access to people's intentions, just their expressions. We can gain an appreciation of the approach that hermeneutics takes to meaning by looking at one specific example, that of legal judgements. This helps us to start to think about what we mean by *the One, the whole, the general, identify* and how these concepts relate dynamically to concepts such as *the many, the parts*, the *specific*, and *difference*.

One of the greatest issues relating to moral behaviour is the tension which exists between knowing what is right in general and knowing what is morally right in any single particular situation. When making decisions about what is morally right, we depend on knowledge of what is right in order to make a particular decision, but at the time of making the decision we often find that there are no universal single rules which can be applied independently of that particular situation. For this reason we need wisdom to guide us between the *general* and the *particular*. This dynamic can be found operating in legal judgments.[84] We cannot codify the law, however clearly it is written, because there will always be a need for discretionary decision-making. We need judges to make legal judgments and juries to decide matters of fact. This opens up the possibility of laws being applied either too leniently or too strictly, resulting in those who are guilty being acquitted of crimes on technicalities while others who are innocent or who have acted out of a genuine moral and ethical obligation are given sentences that the public consider to be far too severe.

Traditional interpretations of Plato emphasise a two-world-view of reality, where the *Ideas* are discrete entities having their existence in a world separate from the material world that we know through our senses. In this new, alternative view of Plato the *Ideas* are not seen as existing in a transcendental world, but in our human world, the one that we experience and which we inhabit, meaning that one idea can only ever be meaningful due to its relationships with other ideas. The implication is that we end up losing an absolute definition of each idea, but what we gain is a deeper sensitivity to a more intuitive dynamic experience of wholeness, with more awareness of how the meaning of ideas and concepts blend together.

Some writers have referred to the *Ideas* as 'transcendentals'. The reason that they were called transcendental is that they relate to those elements of 'Being' which are common to all beings. The transcendentals include being, the One and the many, identity and difference, the beautiful, the good, and truth. We should not think about these transcendentals as separate discrete entities, but as fully interconnected and inseparable. As Wachterhauser explains:

> Gadamer thinks of Platonic Ideas as a nexus or web of ideal relationships, which are internally connected to each other in inseparable ways and at many different levels. Ideas are like strands of thread in a woven cloth…. They exist and function like strands, i.e. like Ideas, only in their interconnectedness in the warp and woof of the fabric…. The multidimensional nexus of relationships with which such ideal aspects of reality present us can only be unravelled a few threads at a time. Thus our understanding of reality is always a selective analysis and explanation, a partial "un-weaving and reweaving" of various parts of the fabric. It is in other words, nothing but "interpretation".[85]

What it means to think, the meaning of thought itself, involves entering this fabric of relations – of un-weaving and reweaving the cloth – in order to discover how these various strands are individually and collectively related to each other. Such thinking involves 'interpretation' because it is never a wordless intuition of the whole. In Plato's *Statesman* we see many discussions of this weaving in relation to a discussion on the nature of 'statesmanship' and 'kingship':

> For this is the single and complete task of kingly weaving-together, never to allow moderate dispositions to stand away from the courageous. Rather, by working them closely into each other as if with a shuttle, through sharing of opinions, through honours, dishonour, esteem, and the giving of pledges to one another, it draws together a a smooth and 'fine-woven' fabric out of them, as the expression is, and always entrusts offices in cities to these in common.[86]

Gadamer encourages us to explore the transcendentals by contemplating the way in which beauty, truth and the good are interwoven and 'belong together' while still attempting to distinguish them. As he wrote in *Truth and Method,* "the Beautiful reveals itself in the search for the Good".[87] The beautiful "attends" and "announces" the truth while never reaching an infallible definition of the truth. Another aspect of beauty which Gadamer highlights is the idea that within beauty there is integrity, and therefore beauty has a moral role to play within our lives, since beauty "challenges us to make our adherence to ethical principles as harmonious, as thought out and integrated into who we are as a beautiful thing is integrated in itself".[88]

In *Holonomics* we introduce readers to the dynamic conception of wholeness. The reason we refer to the conception of wholeness as dynamic is that in order to understand a whole, there is a movement back and forth between the whole and the parts. Gadamer referred to this movement as a "hermeneutic movement" and it is often described as the 'hermeneutic circle'. We can understand this movement if we think about the way in which we understand a written piece of text. When we read, we construe or construct the meaning of a part of a sentence, paragraph or text by already having some overall sense of the whole meaning. As we read we hold within us an expectation of the whole meaning, until that point at which the whole is truly grasped. However, we must always be open to reconstructing the meaning if the text that we are reading demands it.[89]

This same hermeneutical approach to understanding a text can also be applied in relation to understanding works of art. This idea is that we can find a certain form of truth in art, a form of truth that we cannot find in a scientific approach to our understanding of our experience of the world. If we do come to see art as having a legitimate claim to truth, then we will be motivated to study art and to understand it correctly. However, there is an interesting hermeneutical contradiction, which is that if we are to be able to understand art correctly, we have to understand ourselves, something which we can only do through art, since it is art and not science that we are able to explore the question of *being*, what it means to say that something *is*.[90]

In chapter three we explored the transition of consciousness and the journey through the four elements. If we are to understand experience, we need to be able to think of our products and services as artists do, as works of art, and so we have to have the courage to open ourselves to experiencing the world in new and at times ways that are alien to us. Gadamer's philosophical hermeneutics is an exploration of the way in which we experience the world, how we experience art, the way that language discloses reality to us, and the interconnected tapestry of the transcendentals. It is an approach which can bring us much closer to an understanding of the meaning of our products and services, the lived experience of our customers, and the way in which this meaning is living, never completed, always open to an expansion of meaning and being.

This approach is not analytical – it is contemplative, derived through dialogue, both with people *and* with works of art. Hermeneutics breaks us out of our Cartesian understanding of a work, where we have a subject-object relationship, and into the experiencing of the work of art as an event. According to Gadamer, a work of art only fully exists in it being experienced:

> When a work of art truly takes hold of us, it is not an object that stands opposite us which we look at in the hope of seeing through it to an intended conceptual meaning. Just the reverse. The work is an event that "appropriates us" into itself. It jolts us, it knocks us over, and sets up a world of its own, into which we are drawn, as it were.[91]

Gadamer explained hermeneutics as "the art of reaching an understanding" – either of some thing or with someone.[92] This reaching of an understanding is always an interpretation, which happens in conversation, in dialogue. It is for this reason that the outer circle of the holonomic circle contains the transcendentals, a guiding set of ideas which we can use to explore, contemplate and talk about our products, services and customer experiences (Figure 6).

In most working environments we do not often think about why it is that we have the experiences which we do, and how we participate in reality and interpret the world. By taking this more philosophical approach to customer experience design, we can ask questions such as '*is there an objective reality out there waiting to be discovered?*' or '*do we each inhabit a subjective reality with no meaning?*' If we are to really understand customer experiences and how customers are interpreting our products, services and brands, we need to develop new organs of perception, and explore the way in which language and reality *belong together*.

In contemplating the transcendentals we move away from a focus on the tools and techniques used in the design of the customer experience, and into experience itself. This deeper contemplation of the whole and the parts, identity and difference, beauty, truth, goodness, justice and being takes us to a higher level of understanding, and into the lived experience of people and to customer experiences with soul.

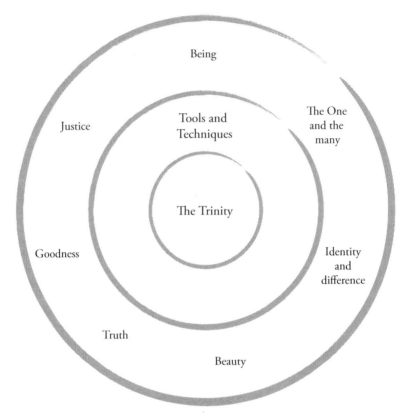

Figure 6: The Holonomic Circle – The Transcendentals

The One and the Many

In the last few decades we have experienced a rapid acceleration in innovation without a parallel acceleration in an appreciation of being. This acceleration has reached a point where biotechnology laboratories are now exploring how we can not only genetically modify plants and animals, but also ourselves as human beings. We can start to create a schematic of this situation by putting 'being' on an axis which is orthogonal to 'doing' (Figure 7).

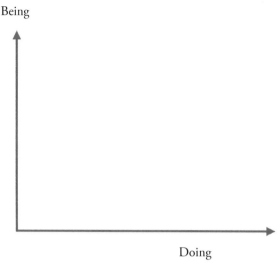

Figure 7: Being – Doing

We have sat through many technology presentations on the future and what is coming which focus almost exclusively on the 'doing' axis – i.e. the focus is on the new technology being created. These presentations, at times bombastic, are often quite light in relation to reflecting on how this can impact on our own human sense of being. While we do need to acknowledge that the word 'consciousness' can be used in many different ways and is therefore problematic, for the purpose of our schematic we can think of the 'doing' dimension as related to innovation, and the 'being' dimension related to consciousness.

We created our simple schematic of 'being and doing' to help entrepreneurs and business leaders to reflect on what exactly they are doing, and why. These reflections are, of course, always framed within a discussion of human values. When we plot 'doing' against 'being' in this way, we can ask ourselves if in fact what we are doing is innovating purely for the sake of innovation, or is what we are doing contributing to an authentic form of human evolution which can only emerge when we develop both our technologies and a deeper sense of being (Figure 8).

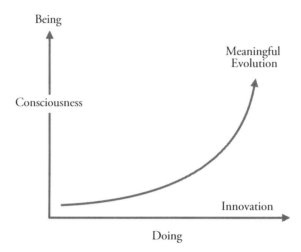

Figure 8: Meaningful Innovation

In philosophy the great question of 'being' is referred to as 'ontology'. An example of an ontological approach to being in business comes from Alex Osterwalder's Business Model Canvas.[93] In 2004, a few years before he began to co-create the canvas with colleagues, Osterwalder wrote a masters thesis titled *The Business Model Ontology: A Proposition in Design Science Approach.*[94] Osterwalder asked the deceptively simply question, "What is a business model?" Taking an ontological approach allowed Osterwalder to tackle the complexities inherent in the concept of business models in order to create a business tool which would facilitate the coordination of a large number of stakeholders, such as partners, strategists, business process designers and information systems staff.

While the dimension of time is contained within the 'doing' dimension, the 'being' dimension in our schematic is less a quantitative graduation and more a journey into being. Osterwalder used the term ontology in relation to developing "a rigorous conceptual model of business models".[95] However, if we take our inspiration from philosophers such as Heidegger and Gadamer, we can learn to expand our consciousness and quality of thinking to develop a deeper sense of being.

We can begin to understand being in a more dynamic manner by thinking about the being of a play such as Hamlet. Starting with Richard Burbage, the first actor to ever portray Hamlet at Shakespeare's Globe Theatre, there have been many great actors who have taken on this role, including Jude Law, Christopher Walken, Ralph Fiennes, David Tennant, Kenneth Branagh, Richard Burton, Laurence Olivier. One of the most recent stagings was in August 2015 which saw huge throngs of fans packed into the Barbican in London to see Benedict Cumberbatch as a hoodie-wearing Hamlet, directed and interpreted by Lyndsey Turner. At one and the same time, it is possible to conceive of there being the One Hamlet, and many Hamlets. Each new version of Hamlet is not a copy of the previous Hamlet, nor is it totally different and unrelated to the previous Hamlet. We recognise each authentic performance as being Hamlet (the One) while also being different from other Hamlets (the many).[96]

If we ask the question *'What is the being of a play?'*, it is not that a play exists just as a script, as words on paper. It partially exists in this format, but this is not the fullest expression of its being. Neither does a play fully exist in the head of the playwright, which actors, directors and other members of a production team try to recreate, and neither does it fully exist in the minds of the audience who are watching the play. In asking what a play is, as well as pointing to the elements which make up a play – the script, the actors, the costumes, the set, the theatre, the director, the audience – we can also conceive of the being of a play as being at its fullest in the performance of the play. When we experience an authentic interpretation of a play we experience it as a whole, where all the parts belong together, giving us a great sense of wonder, excitement and fulfilment. When a play is badly performed, we are so distracted by what is wrong with it, that it is not able to present itself to us.

By thinking of the 'being' as the 'happening' of the performing, we move away from thinking about the play in an intellectual sense, in terms of the meaning of the actors, director, audience members etc., towards developing an intuitive connection with the very essence of a play; we move upstream into experiencing the play *playing*. This is the dynamic conception of wholeness, the whole play being experienced as it comes to presence through the parts, which in each performance can always grow, and expand in meaning, while always remaining whole. The meaning of 'play' from this perspective is always unfinished, since the dynamic conception of wholeness allows for an expansion of meaning without losing the sense of wholeness. The reason that we coined the phrase *'customer experiences with soul'* was to help people make an intuitive leap from understanding their purpose to understanding how this purpose comes to presence in products and services. We experience products and (especially) services as counterfeit when people in an organisation are not able to allow the purpose to play them, due to a lack of resonance, understanding and leadership.

We encounter counterfeit brands with counterfeit purposes when what the brand says, what the brand means and what the brand does fail to coalesce as a unified whole. The example of the play can help us to develop an understanding of being, but there are essential differences between the being of a play, in which actors aim to remove their personalities to become a new character, and an authentic purpose which empowers people to bring their whole selves to work, fulfilled in meaningful work for the betterment of society and the planet. Ironically, one of the situations which most raises our ire is when we encounter people in a call centre who are not acting as fully human, but as machines who have to mechanically follow a linear script which more often than not does not match our reason for calling. Customers can sense an inauthentic performance of services, but they are delighted when people fully embody the spirit of an organisation (identity) without losing a sense of who they are as an individual (difference). When a purpose is truly authentic, there is no difference in the way in which this purpose is expressed in the behaviours, speech and actions of those who believe in it.

Identity and Difference

In the 1990s, the port of Recife in the north of Brazil had the highest unemployment rate in the country. In response to the harsh living conditions, a number of musicians resolved to transform the city away from all the crime, poverty and unemployment there. The new musical movement which emerged was known as 'Mangue Bit', a name inspired by the mangrove swamps from the region, and the new digital world.[97] The word 'bit' is an imported word into Portuguese and, when spoken in Portuguese, 'bit' sounds like the English word 'beat', and so there is an additional play on words. The popularity of the movement would lead to the transformation of the vision and image which Recife had of itself, as well as the culture of the surrounding regions.

The musicians discussed diversity in terms of modern musical styles such as rock and hip hop, as well as the traditional musical styles from the north east, especially *maracatu*, a percussive style with its roots in African slave culture. Since the majority of the musicians from Recife did not have the financial resources to leave the city, they resolved to create something new. New bands formed from groups of friends who attended the early parties which were hosted in the derelict but cheap docks, including Fred Zero Quatro who was the leader of the group Mundo Livre ('Free World'), which had been formed in the 1980s, with influences from both The Clash and samba.

In 1992 Fred Zero Quatro co-wrote the Mangue Bit manifesto, which was titled *Crabs with Brains*. It starts with a reflection on the diversity of life found in mangroves, and how mangroves are among the most productive ecosystems in the world, being symbolic of fertility, diversity and richness. This is then followed by a potent analysis of the city, which in the previous thirty years had succumbed to extreme poverty and urban chaos. The final section of the manifesto is the call to action to revitalise both town and the natural environment:

Emergency! Get the paramedics or Recife dies of a heart attack. The quickest way to kill and empty the soul of a city is
to kill its rivers and to fill its estuaries. How to avoid drown-
ing in the chronic depression that paralyses the citizens? It's
simple, just inject some energy into the mud, and stimulate
what's left of the fertility in the veins of Recife. Dream up an
energy circuit capable of connecting the positive vibrations
of the mangroves with the world wide web. The symbol, a
parabolic antenna rammed into the mud.[98]

The key figure of the Mangue Bit movement was Chico Science,
born in 1966, who along with his band Nação Zumbi (Zombi
Nation) transformed *maracatu*. "The city never stops, the city just
keeps growing, the top rises and the bottom sinks" he sang in the
song *A Cidade* ('The City'). For Chico, the idea was to take regional
rhythms and add to them, creating a new style and genre, mixing
the regional and the universal. One of the characteristics of Mangue
Bit was that every artist had a different style. Within the movement
it was not possible to discern an aesthetic unity binding the factions
together. Mangue Bit celebrated difference.

In the 1990s, consultants at Andersen Consulting used to be
referred to as 'Anderoids', a nickname which was inspired by the
general perception within the industry which saw people working for
the consultancy as clones, adhering to the strict conformity of their
corporate culture. While corporate cultures can result in homogene-
ity, artistically-driven cultures such as Mangue Bit have the power to
change our way of seeing, both the proponents of the movement and
those outside of the movement looking in. Cultural manifestos such
as *Crabs with Brains* are not about creating rigid uniformity across all
members; they are about connecting members with the essence, sensing the deeper unity of what unites the group, tribe or organisation.

Our ways of seeing can be so deeply ingrained in us that it often takes an inspired leader or an industry outsider to show us the

full potential reach of our current products and services. Fernando Peire is on the Board of Caprice Holdings and is Director of The Ivy restaurant and private room, and The Club at The Ivy. In each episode of the Channel 5 series *The Restaurant Inspector,* Peire visits a failing restaurant to offer his expert advice to the owners on what is wrong and what they should do. This is a wonderful example of the dynamics of seeing in action, showing the contrasting ways in which Peire perceives the restaurants from the owners. His approach is entirely from the perspective of the clientele, something which the owners often struggle to understand:

> Peire takes an almost paternal, nurturing interest in both the restaurant and The Club. For him, it is always about creating the right atmosphere, the right ambience, so that the particular Ivy magic can emerge. How does he describe what makes the Ivy special? "It's the conversation. The Ivy is all about conversation. When you read about The Ivy, people talk about the buzz. I'm very proud of our staff too – they are an integral part of The Ivy. But it's people talking to each other – even married couples talking to each other...[99]

Restaurants are, of course, incredibly sensory experiences, and in São Paulo we discovered an enchanting street which epitomises the way in which an owner of a restaurant understands the experience of the clientele in relation to the dynamic relationship between the whole and parts, and of identity and difference. Rua Avanhandava (Avanhandava Street) lies in the heart of São Paulo. In 1980 Walter Mancini opened the first Famiglia Mancini restaurant but his vision was greater than just one single restaurant. His vision was to renovate the entire street, the first project of its kind in São Paulo.[100]

It is not just the restaurants which people come to visit; a stroll down the street is an experience in itself, with Mancini describing it as "festive and joyful. This whole range of colours, this multifaceted is really what makes this street so unique". The street is home to five restaurants and two shops, and the experience for visitors begins at the very entrance, which comes into its own at night with the coloured street lights and two fountains, as Mancini says:

> I feel very happy and fulfilled in knowing that I've been slowly building all that is here, and that this work brings happiness to people.

The first restaurant on the street is Pizza and Pasta Mancini, an elegant building consisting of the main hall, a mezzanine floor and a balcony which between them have 300 seats. It hosts live music and is home to two baby grand pianos, as well as fountains both inside and outside. Opposite is Migalhas, a bakery and cafe selling fresh bread and serving sandwiches, burgers and draft beers. Next to Migalhas is Madreperola, a sea food restaurant which is packed so full of antique nautical memorabilia, curiosities and maritime themed works of art that it feels as if you have been transported onto the set of a European cult film. A wooden tattooed mermaid draped in necklaces, for example, hangs by fishing nets from the ceiling, with a patch over one eye, wearing a pirate hat and flippers.

The most famous restaurant, Famiglia Mancini, sees queues of people waiting for a table every single day of the week. The restaurant has been created and developed by Mancini since 1980 with great love, devotion and enthusiasm. He describes it as having "the finger of God, a magical house". The details are astounding; it is truly an enchanting experience of near sensory overload, not only with walls packed with artefacts – cheeses, meats, paintings, bottles, jars, jugs, copper pans, works of art – but the ceilings as well. The centre-piece is a small alcove named their 'sanctuary', where two small tables sit either side of a tiled fountain. The sanctuary is festooned in honour of all the saints, angels and gods "that help us here", and it can indeed feel more like a pilgrimage than a trip to an Italian restaurant.

In addition to Calligraphia, a gallery and art shop, and Gato Bravo, a shop selling vintage clothes and other collectible items, there is also Il Ristaurante, a high-class restaurant famous for its mission to offer "the best live music in town". Along the top of the bar are hundreds of plaques with the names of all the national and internationally famous musicians who have played at the restaurant. Next to a clock is a special plaque which has the inscription, "In homage of gratitude to all the musicians who with their art contributed to the success of this house". As Mancini explains, "We don't close, every day we work and the music goes on, without interruption. The music here is very beautiful. It's a very romantic house. At night it is wonderful".

Famiglia Mancini is not simply the totality of the physical parts. There is something more about Famiglia Mancini that we not able to write down, nor touch or feel, but which exists and which we encounter through a sensitive contemplation of each and every detail. This allows us to experience Rua Avanhandava as an authentic whole, where every part *belongs* together, creating an unbroken experience that we can delight in. This sense of wholeness does not come at the price of conformity or standardising the experience across all of the restaurants and shops. Each has its own unique identity while at the same time allowing us to have an enchanting and unbroken experience when we visit Rua Avanhandava.

We can only really grasp this wholeness in our intuition; it is neither rational nor tangible, and so this is why it is important to contemplate the four different ways of knowing: thinking, feeling, sensing and intuition. In this mode of consciousness, experiencing the whole as an 'active absence', we move from the sensory to the intuitive, and in our intuition we discover the *meaning* of Famiglia Mancini. In our modern society, an analytic mode of consciousness has become dominant, leading us to experience ourselves as a spectator, side by side with the objects that we are seeing and the phenomena that we are sensing. As we saw with the example of a play, actors experience a play as an active absence which then starts to move them. Henri Bortoft drew a distinction between this former analytical mode of experience and the receptive mode, in which events are allowed to happen:

> Instead of being verbal, analytical, sequential, and logical, this mode of consciousness is nonverbal, holistic, nonlinear and intuitive. It emphasises sensory and perceptual instead of the rational categories of the action mode. It is based on taking in, rather than manipulating, the environment. If we were re-educated in the receptive mode of consciousness, our encounter with wholeness would be considerably different, and we would see many new things about our world.[101]

It may seem obvious that a restaurant owner understands the experience of the client, but in so many cases this appears not be the case, as it was for us when we went to a restaurant in São Paulo where the staff seemed to be happy to play music from a radio station with intrusive and grating advertisements. The music and noise were highly incongruent with the atmosphere and environment that the owners were clearly aiming for, but when restaurant owners do not have the ability to place themselves in the shoes of their guests it results in people like ourselves leaving to search for another place to dine. It is clear that Mancini's love of art and food, and his continual attention to the experience of his clientele, have resulted in the one of the most delightfully curious and enchanting dining experiences in São Paulo. The Mancini family deserve high praise for their restaurants, creating such a wonderful experience of the parts and the whole for us to explore, contemplate and plunge into.

The dynamic conception of wholeness has been with us since Plato's time, and yet often it has remained disguised and not recognised, because the form in which it appears has been in many different contexts. Gadamer extended hermeneutics to include art, especially performance art, with one of his most powerful examples being the periodic festival:

> The festival that comes around is neither another festival nor a mere remembrance of the one that was originally celebrated.[102]

For Gadamer, there is the one 'festival' which "only exists in being celebrated".[103] This is the question of being. Furthermore, there is a historical or time dimension to the festival, in that each celebration is not the same as the last. The wholeness of the festival is found in its unity and identity; a unity and wholeness which is dynamic, because however much it is transformed and distorted the festival still remains itself. In an organisational context, we can use Gadamer's example of the periodic festival to ask if there is an analogue in business.

Businesses more often than not have Christmas parties, and one potentially interesting piece of research would be an analysis of natural and unposed photographs of different office Christmas parties. What would you see if you looked at photos of your own office parties? Would you observe a healthy and rich range of interactions between people from different departments, sections and teams, with senior management mixing freely and not just with their peers, but also with more junior staff? Or would you see cliques, bunkers and people huddled around according to their social class and status within the organisational hierarchy?

Annual general meetings are normally very staid affairs, with certain rules and regulations to be followed, and are generally attended by those in the financial sector and shareholders with significant holdings. BrewDog, however, have turned on its head the notion of what an AGM can and should be. BrewDog call their AGM "annual general mayhem" – turning their AGM into a festival. The

2016 BrewDog AGM was held in April at the Aberdeen Exhibition and Conference Centre. For several years it has been the largest AGM in the UK, attended by equity punk investors, who have exclusive access to tickets. The demand was so high in 2016 that each investor was only able to bring one guest, with some investors not able to attend due to the event selling out.

Every year it is an all day party, opening at 11.00am and the 2016 gathering started with a business update from James Watt and Martin Dickie. Their presentation was crammed full of jokes at the expense of their competitors and their own staff and, while irreverent, it was also full of passion in their review of what worked in 2015 and also what went wrong, or in their words, "kind of sucked". Watt closed their presentation telling the crowd:

> It's been a fantastic twelve months and the next twelve months promise to be even more exciting. Everything that we've done, we've done together. Everything we've been able to build we've been able to build because you guys have been involved with us. By investing in our business, believing in what we do, you guys have helped turn our industry on its head, and you guys have kick-started a revolution, and that is what Equity for Punks is all about.

The BrewDog AGM is not merely a presentation of their financial results; it is a celebration of who they are. This identify extends from the business to their investors, who are in fact an authentic community of customers. The AGM brings BrewDog far closer to their investors and customers in a way in which social media alone could not achieve. This closeness is not created in the formal physical proximity of a focus group, but in the informal celebration of who they are, united by a single unifying purpose centred around craft beer.

Beauty

> Blessed are they who see beautiful things in humble places
> where other people see nothing.
>
> Camille Pissaro

This quotation is printed on a wall of one of the galleries of the Kelvingrove Art Gallery and Museum in Glasgow, a truly imposing and magnificent landmark building which is home to one of Europe's great art collections. Its most famous and controversial painting is Salvador Dali's *Christ of Saint John of the Cross*. The centrepiece of the dramatic Centre Hall is a concert pipe organ where visitors can hear organ recitals daily at 1pm. The last time we visited, the organist Chris Nickol decided to play David Bowie's *Life on Mars* after hearing of the singer's death on the morning news bulletins, with mobile phone footage of this improvised performance going viral worldwide.

It is not by accident that the Kelvingrove is one of the most visited attractions in Scotland. One of the delights of the museum is the way in which the curators and managers place so much emphasis on the experience of their visitors, including the positioning of some paintings at knee-height so that young children can appreciate the art on their own terms. On a previous visit to the Kelvingrove, not only did we listen to the lunchtime organ recital, but also to some wonderful Scottish folk music in the Scottish Identity in Art gallery, where we even took part, playing percussion, as did some of the other members of the audience there.

One of the core questions explored in the extensive research carried out with visitors and members of the public in the years before the refurbishment was how the museum could provide opportunities for emotional involvement and aesthetic appreciation, as well as more traditional education and knowledge gain. People visit museums not just for educational reasons, but for personal and social reasons too, which can include curiosity, duty, motivations, interests, feelings and social interaction.[104] It is interesting to study the way in which the gallery has been laid out as a result of the insights gained from the research. Having undergone an extensive refurbishment in 2006, the two wings which are to the east and to the west of the Centre Hall were named 'Expression' – how we express ourselves and why we need to, and 'Life' – how we live and what that does to the world. Within each of the twenty-two galleries there are 'story displays' which allow visitors to explore a single exhibit in detail, bringing them to life with interactive elements and carefully crafted questions which are written in accessible and non-academic language while at no time talking down to visitors, be they adults or children.

One of the main galleries is dedicated to The Glasgow Boys, a loose-knit group of Glasgow-based artists who reached a creative peak in the 1880s and 1890s. In The Glasgow Boys we find the same punk attitude as BrewDog, formed out of desire to disrupt the status quo of a staid, safe and boring school of art which was centred around the elitist art schools in Edinburgh. One composition from this collection, *The Druids – Bringing in the Mistletoe*, which was jointly painted by George Henry and Edward Atkinson Hornel in 1890, stands out as being particularly breathtaking (Figure 9). The mistletoe, a plant venerated by druids, can be seen on the heads of the white wild cattle. Henry and Hornel went to great lengths to ensure that this particular ancient breed would have been present in the era of the druids, and they studied the skulls of cattle to ensure as good a likeness as possible. There is something about being up close against the brush-strokes of a great painting that places you in the presence of the artist as no reproduction possibly could.

Figure 9: *The Druids – Bringing in the Mistletoe*,
reproduced courtesy of Glasgow Museums

This painting was a hugely innovative and almost shocking piece of art for its era, ahead of its time, due not only to the flattened perspective, but particularly for the daring and revolutionary use of gold leaf which captivated spectators across Europe. This was especially the case in Germany, where it was exhibited in Munich and declared the most radical painting of its era. When you see this otherworldly painting for the first time, you can easily understand the response of those who viewed it when it was first presented; there is a monumental spirituality in its experience – the wise and focused expression in the druids, the moon-like mound, and the bright colours which have almost never been used to depict druids in this manner. To use Gadamer's words, standing in front of this extraordinary masterpiece one has an extremely vivid sensation. It is a quite extraordinary experience. Having seen this painting on two previous occasions, you can imagine our disappointment when we returned to the Kelvingrove in 2016, only to be told by a guide that the painting was out on loan to a gallery in Sweden.

On our annual visit back to the UK, in January 2016 we had one final day in London before heading back to Brazil, and out of all the things we could have done we decided to visit the British Museum. On arrival, we discovered that one of the exhibitions was about the Celts, and so we decided to view this one. We entered the exhibition, which was one the greatest displays of Celtic relics and artworks to have been put on public display, including the Desborough Mirror. As we gradually made our way around the exhibition, seeing incredible artefacts such as a magical cauldron, jewellery, arms, crosses, clothes and pottery, all with incredibly intricate Celtic designs, we caught sight of the painting we so longed to see. There, on the wall, in all its glory was *The Druids – Bringing in the Mistletoe*. It was an amazing experience to discover this painting once more, and what a chance encounter it was, totally unexpected. Perhaps we heard it calling to us so that we could admire it once more, surrounded by so much Celtic art which inspired its creators.

In his hermeneutical enquiries, Gadamer saw an approach in Plato which brought out the phenomenon of the beautiful, and the way in which beauty was likened to 'radiance':

> "Radiance," then, is not only one of the qualities of the beautiful but constitutes its actual being. The distinguishing mark of the beautiful – namely that it immediately attracts the human soul to it – is founded in its mode of being. "To shine" means to shine on something, and so to make that on which the light falls appear. Beauty has the mode of being of light.[105]

Gadamer felt that Plato's metaphysics still had something relevant to teach us today about the truth and the way in which truth has an ability to present itself through beauty:

> Thus the beautiful is distinguished from the absolutely intangible good in that it can be grasped. It is part of its own nature to be something that is visibly manifest. The beautiful reveals itself in the search for the good.[106]

Gadamer was concerned with the limitations of the scientific method in relation to claims about the truth, especially in relation to the logical empiricism of the Vienna Circle, which took hold in the early part of the twentieth century. Prior to Gadamer, Goethe published his *Theory of Colours* in 1810, a treatise which also concerned itself with the limitations of the scientific method and the way in which the focus was on a codification of light in the form of abstract lines and geometry and not on the actual phenomena of colour itself. At that moment in the history of science, no other scientist or philosopher was more fully versed in the study and knowledge of colour than Goethe, a polymath poet, artist and scientist. No other person had undertaken such an in-depth investigation into colour, and yet he was roundly ridiculed and rejected. Goethe, like Gadamer, believed that we could access a form of truth through developing an artistic and aesthetic form of consciousness, grounded in phenomena.

In *Holonomics* we write extensively about Goethe's theory of colour and explain how it can be explored using glass prisms. We often introduce these exercises into our classes, lectures and workshops, and it always proves to be an extremely powerful experience for those taking part. The reason is that our intellects are not on their own able to fully grasp what Goethe is teaching us about how to explore the phenomenological nature of the natural world. Goethe developed a complementary way of science which he hoped would achieve a deeper way of understanding nature by plunging into our senses.

This approach fully trusts our senses to explore natural phenomena, rather than the modern scientific stance which distrusts our senses as purely subjective, without meaning and, therefore, secondary to any quantifiable way of reducing nature to measures:

> He, to whom nature begins to unveil her open secrets, feels an irresistible longing for her worthiest interpreter, art.[107]

At the precociously young age of 21, Rudolf Steiner (1861–1925) started to edit the scientific papers of Goethe, a project that would last for many years. As a young boy he had had many spiritual experiences, and this would lead him to becoming involved in the German Theosophical Society. In 1912, Steiner broke away from theosophy to set up the Anthroposophical Society, based on his philosophy inspired by Goethe and which he thought would lead to the evolution of human consciousness and access to spiritual knowledge. His ambition was to take art and elevate it to the level of spiritual science. The scientific instrument that Steiner used was the human imagination, using our imagination experientially:

> The imagination is a fine and beautiful instrument, but we must experiment with it if we want to discover this for ourselves.[108]

Through an intuitive understanding of colour, Steiner expanded on Goethe's theory by introducing the distinction between 'active' colours and 'passive' colours. Black, white, green and peach-blossom were 'picture' or 'image' colours – in that they were pictures of something – the living, the soul, the spirit. Yellow, blue and red were termed 'lustre' colours in that "something shines from them".[109] In terms of understanding the concept of 'shining', we could not reach an understanding through an intellectual and abstract understanding, but rather through feeling. Steiner elevated feelings to objective reality, and in terms of the lustre colours he came to the conclusion that yellow was the lustre of the spirit, blue was the lustre of soul and red was the lustre of the living:

> The artist knows that when he handles yellow, blue and red he must induce in his picture something that expresses an inwardly dynamic quality which gives itself character. If he is working with peach-blossom and green on black or white then he knows that an image quality is already present in the colour. Such a science of colour is so inwardly living that it can pass immediately from the soul's experience into art.[110]

Steiner's ultimate ambition was to demonstrate with rigorous methodological validity that colour had a hidden nature which we could only discover when we developed a sensitivity to working within feeling. Even at the time of writing in 1921, he thought that in placing so much emphasis on abstract mathematics his age had "actually lost that living element of soul".[111] Exploring artistic consciousness dramatically alters our relationships to others in our lives; it changes our comportment and values, and reaches down into our very being, taking us from counterfeit to authentic ways of living sustainably and mindfully.

Eduardo Srur is one of the world's leading urban interventionists, designing large scale works of art in urban spaces, which draw people's attention to the environment and major issues affecting cities and urban living. His book *Manual de Intervenção Urbana* (Urban Intervention Manual), published in 2012, illustrates sixteen years of his projects and works. He graduated in art from the faculty of plastic art at Armando Alvares Penteado Foundation (FAAP) in 1997, one of the most important and respected academic institutions in Brazil, created with the objective of supporting, promoting and developing the plastic and scenic arts, culture and teaching. Eduardo started to experiment with painting, video, sculpture, photography, performance while also taking a further degree in Publicity, also at FAAP.

We had the chance to catch up with Eduardo at his studio in São Paulo where we discussed art, sustainability, leadership and transition. He founded the São Paulo-based company Attack Intervençóes Urbanas and has worked in partnership with many leading brands. His interest in the many different forms of expression in the plastic arts lead him to explore how he could use their varying and different languages in public spaces. In our conversation Eduardo discussed the way in which he found the contemporary art scene restrictive for artists in many different ways, sentiments which echo those of the Glasgow Boys, and so he realised that by working in large public spaces he could reach a wider public:

> This is how the idea of 'urban interventions' was born. At the time there was no established term for it. Nowadays it is a known term 'urban interventions' defined as 'an artistic form of expression in public spaces for a temporary time'. So the difference with public art is that it is temporary, unlike a bronze statue which is permanent. Art only for the sake of art does not make sense. It has to transform.

Eduardo describes ATTACK as being at "the cutting-edge of art and publicity". He makes a distinction between his art and his entrepreneurial projects, since he has two distinct roles, that of an artist and that of a person helping organisations which seek him. When companies ask him to produce something, the works which are created are not totally his, but they are "a new way to interact with people". Often his projects are initiated by people inside the organisations who realise and value the contributions Eduardo can bring to a creative project.

> Today companies can no longer just seek profit, they need a cultural and social role. Companies who do not have these

cultural and social dimensions will start to be criticised heavily by clients.

He does not have a single formula for success, since he is always inciting himself to do something new and different. The ultimate aim is always the same, to provoke people and transform their imagination, breaking them out of their daily experience of urban life:

> People are anaesthetised – an artist has to provoke and make people reflect. A city is a gallery. A public space can be a gallery. It is an amplified blank canvas where I have more power to be creative; there are more possibilities. I have more space to act, it is more democratic and I can seek out society so that people can participate and interact with the projects, which more and more are collaborative. Nowadays an artist is not marginalised, he or she is accepted in modern society, because an artist has the mission to amplify the consciousness of people, helping them to see reality in a different form. Artists have to have the responsibility to understand themselves as professionals, but they need other professionals to create projects of this magnitude. The power and energy is in the artist's concept, which provokes people. So nowadays it is a collaborative act in order to be able to materialise their idea. As an artist you can never be satisfied with reality. You always have to question things. You have to have conviction in yourself, create your own poetry and form of expression.

Eduardo made the point that artists do not just have the ability to paint or sculpt well. They also have an ability to communicate a concept, and this leads to the expansion of consciousness and new ways of seeing:

An expansion of consciousness for me is related to the maximum connection with yourself, with your intuition, your field of senses, your thoughts and your feelings. You are integral and whole, and knowing that you are not inventing the wheel, you are using elements around you and re-arranging them. For example you have free words and depending on how you arrange them you can create a poem. So an expansion of consciousness is how you re-arrange the things around you. The idea of transformation and expansion of consciousness, comes from the idea of simplicity, things which are in our hands. I was always an artist who always dealt with things which were close to me. With this idea of simplicity anyone can be an artist, having an ability to transform reality. You are giving a new meaning to those things around you.

In Eduardo we discover an artist who is able to stay within his artistic consciousness while at the same time managing to engage with global brands and help them understand how his urban interventions can contribute authentically to their efforts to change people's consciousness, awareness and patterns of consumption. This changing awareness comes from the ability of art to knock us temporarily out of our normal unconscious daily patterns of thinking, forcing us to momentarily contemplate the unexpected. This is why urban interventions are so important, as there is no avoiding the shock of what we encounter in what are normally very familiar locations where we are often on auto-pilot. It is interesting to look at the growing trend which is seeing people moving away from an obsession with new products, gadgets and the accumulation of 'stuff', and towards seeking out novel and meaningful experiences. Ultimately, every interaction with a product such a smart phone or watch or even something as mundane as a kitchen knife is an experience, but the shift into an 'experience economy' is characterised by the way in which people are actively seeking out new and unique sensory experiences, for example, restaurants in which we eat while blindfolded.

Holonomic thinking is such a powerful approach to customer experience design because it fully integrates artistic vision and consciousness into our conception of how we make sense of the world, how we explain our place in the world and how we relate to others, both other people and our environment. By exploring artistic consciousness, even if we do not consider ourselves to have any artistic abilities or sensibilities, we can discover something about both ourselves and others that can allow us to implement more effective, sustainable, transformational and soulful customer experiences in whichever organisation we may be working.

Truth

> It is a Sufi contention that truth is not discovered or maintained by the mere repetition of teachings. It can only be kept understood by the perpetual experience of it. And it is in the experience of truth that the Sufis have always reposed their trust. Sufism is not therefore "Do as I say and not as I do" or even "Do as I do", but "Experience it and you will know".[112]
>
> Idries Shah

This quotation from Idries Shah is alerting us to the limitations of language and the need to understand the relationship between language, statements, propositions, commands and experience. It is not without reason that half of *Holonomics* is dedicated to the dynamics of seeing, since we often do not dedicate time to thinking about experience, what experience is, how we experience the world, how other people experience the world, how our experience of the world may differ from others and, ultimately, how we can access truth through experience. If you are a chief executive of a construction company in Brazil, your reality will be extremely different from that of a school teacher in Colombia, who will have an extremely different reality from a banker on Wall Street, who will have an extremely different reality from a plasterer in Britain, who will have an extremely different reality from a tailor in India. It is not too difficult to think about these different realities and to understand intellectually that they are different, but to what extent can we really walk in the shoes of another and really know about their lives? Social, tribal, economic, cultural, age and personal life events are just a few factors which make a difference to our lived experiences, but behind all of these lies the fundamental role of language.

In general, there have been two contrasting approaches and ideas about the relationship between language and reality. The first is what Brice Wachterhauser calls 'linguistic constructivism' where "language is the means by which we construct or impute meaning to reality".[113] The second, 'alinguistic essentialism' by contrast suggests that the intelligibility of reality "consists in its ideal, alinguistic structure which the mind can intuit without any necessary reliance on language".[114] Gadamer's general strategy in *Truth and Method* was to argue that language and reality belong together, seeing language as the place where thought and reality meet.[115] To say that language and reality belong together means that language is an indispensable place where the intelligibility of what is real makes itself manifest. Language "participates" making reality intelligible, but at the same time it is the intelligibility of reality which "participates" in the intelligibility of language.

Gadamer famously said that "being that can be understood is language".[116] Our experience of the world can be limited by our particular use and understanding of language, be it due to which language it is (English, Portuguese, Chinese etc.) and the language of our professions, specialist academic subjects, peer groups, social class etc. The intelligibility of the world is reflected in language. Language, Gadamer argued, is like light in that it has the ability to make things visible to us without itself becoming visible.[117] Through language, phenomena are at one and the same time unconcealed, made manifest to us, but also concealed or covered over. An example of this is the way in which some people have an over-reliance on technical language, ending up with only a partial understanding of a topic or discipline.

One of the greatest problems organisations face is that we as people are convinced that the way we see reality is the right and only way. We very rarely contemplate the fact that other people can have profoundly different experiences of reality, ways of making sense of the world and understanding complex situations and problems in dramatically different ways. In order to facilitate the introduction of discussions about truth into organisations, we created *The Ladder of Seeing* which is a simple but powerful tool to help executives evaluate both their own ways of seeing and those of others (Figure 10).[118]

Figure 10: The Ladder of Seeing

A creative organisation infused with holonomic thinking has leaders who are able to make effective decisions and find powerful solutions, which emerge not from one person's mental models and paradigms dominating others, but through capturing the rich diversity of people's different ways of thinking and seeing.[119] This can only come about through genuine dialogue. The statement of the ladder is "We see", but this should not be interpreted as 'groupthink'. When we see together, we have a level of maturity which avoids the need to arrive at a single truth or absolute certainty.

The Greek word *logos* contains within it a variety of meanings, including *account, principle, reason, ratio, discourse* and *theory*.[120] A *logos* can be something very simple, such as a shared in-joke between colleagues, or something more complicated, such as a theoretical perspective or a philosophical foundation for research such as positivism, realism and interpretivism. We can think of an individual *logos* as a 'whole of meaning' – a whole which is limited, only relating to one subject matter or issue, and yet also living in the sense of being porous, open to the world and other spheres of discourse.

Gadamer characterised the *logoi* as always being in constant interaction with other *logoi*. Unlike Descartes who took the idea that a proposition could be self-contained and fully understandable in isolation, without any reference to other propositions, Gadamer saw speech as living, always being open to new meanings and change. Ultimately this approach to language means that we can never know reality as a whole, since we can only know reality through the *logoi*.[121] But if we come back to the question of humility, we can now see why it is such a powerful quality to have, especially for leaders. When we are humble, we are able to accept that our own access to reality, through language, while on the one hand being limited, does not limit us to having access to truth about the world. If we have a degree of humility, we have an ability to ascend the ladder of seeing by having genuine dialogue those with whom we have contact.

We formulated this simple set of guidelines for those people wishing to instigate authentic dialogue in their organisations:[122]

Avoid having a leader of the discussion.
Avoid abstracting, judging, and defending.
Do not treat conversations as competitions with a winner.
Honour other people's mental models.
Feel a part of the whole group.
Trust in solutions which emerge from the whole dialogue.

In his message to future generations in 1959, Bertrand Russell said that when studying any matter, or considering any philosophy, "Ask yourself only what are the facts, and what is the truth that the facts bear out. Never let yourself be diverted either by what you wish to believe, or by what you think would have beneficent social effects if it were believed. Look only and solely on what are the facts".[123] The transcendentals in the holonomic circle draw our attention to a very different approach to the truth, one which places primacy on the question rather than the answer. Brice Wachterhauser describes this idea in the following manner:

If one wants to grasp its truth there is no proposition that can be comprehended solely from the content it presents. Every proposition is motivated. Every proposition has presuppositions that it does not express. Only they who comprehend these presuppositions can really judge the truth of a proposition. Now I maintain that the ultimate logical form of such motivation of every proposition is the question. It is not the judgement that has logical priority but the question as is historically attested by the Platonic dialogue and dialectical origin of Greek logic. The primacy of the question over against the proposition implies, however, that the proposition is essentially an answer. There is no proposition that does not represent a type of answer.[124]

The holonomic circle teaches us to develop a more refined notion of what facts actually are and how we interpret them. There is a huge difference between the proposition 'our product is easy to use' and the question 'is our product easy to use?' For example, a department such as marketing may have its own truth and reality, and another department, such as innovation or research and development may have a very different truth. Customer experiences with soul are created by unified cultures which promote curiosity and questioning, a style of working which requires people to keep multiple and conflicting hypotheses open at the same time, and also to be able to explore reality from many angles and perspectives. These cultures can only exist when human values are operating, allowing authentic dialogue and creative conversation to take place.

Customer experiences with soul emerge naturally from organisations who live the universal human values of peace, truth, love, righteousness and non-violence. We will never understand the experience of our customers if we remain welded to a static and singular way of constructing and experiencing reality, living lives full of competitive conversations which are simply exchanges of dogmatically held beliefs, the outcome of which is a winning proposition and the exclusion of all others. Exploring the interweaving nexus of the transcendentals dialectically opens us to an ever-changing vista of viewpoints and interpretations where beauty, truth and goodness all belong together within our experience.

Goodness

Thomas Kolster is the author of *Goodvertising: Creative Adverting that Cares* and the founder of the Goodvertising advertising agency, helping clients to put purpose into their brands. Thomas's work is based around three questions; can advertising be a force for good, can it bring around positive social and environmental change, and should advertising tell the truth about brands? He describes 'goodvertising' as a different marketing model which is "not based on pushing wants but solving needs" and where brands develop a bigger vision to solve some of society's biggest problems for people as opposed to creating false desires.

We have known Thomas for a number of years, and in October 2016 we had the opportunity to meet up to discuss Goodvertising in depth. Thomas started out as a copywriter in the advertising industry, but two separate factors were to lead him to shift his focus from selling to seeing brands as a force for good. The first was the influence of his parents, who both of whom were teachers and never great fans of advertising, leading Thomas to never feel totally comfortable in his work, despite having all the trappings of a successful and glamorous career. Thomas is Danish, and the second factor was COP 15 which took place in Copenhagen, Denmark in December 2009. Thomas recalled that at that time "people thought we were going to pull it off [COP 15], it was in Copenhagen in Denmark. That was my moment where I have to do something about this".

At that time there were very few marketing campaigns based around doing good, and so Thomas interviewed many leading names in advertising, media and design to explore the hypothesis that brands which do good also benefit the bottom line. While his book *Goodvertising* received critical acclaim when it was published in 2012, Thomas still worries that "maybe I am not doing good enough, maybe I am doing the opposite". The reason for this is that important ethical considerations come into play in relation to helping brands to tell a positive story about part of their activities, whereas other parts of their activities remain harmful or questionable, including those activities of their holding companies. For this reason Thomas feels that his work over the last year or so has become more activist in nature, placing an emphasis on the impact of brands' campaigns:

> If you have been in this space for even a short time you just get tired of corporate nonsense. You go into an organisation and it is not anchored anywhere. It is just marketing. And then I don't like it.

We asked Thomas about which companies, brands or campaigns he really thinks epitomise the Goodvertising philosophy, and the examples he gave reflected his developing interest in empowering people and communities. The first example he gave was Wheelys Cafe, a disruptive coffee franchise which is taking on global high street coffee and food chains. Basing their model on the fact that it takes $1 million to open a Starbucks unit, people who wish to become entrepreneurs can open a Wheely's bike cafe for around $6,000. As Thomas remarked:

> It challenges business as usual and it generates real money for people, and we have all worked our way up in organisations where we only do it for the money. If I worked in a coffee shop I would work for the money. If I had my own coffee bike I would work my butt off, I would be passionate, I would love it.

The second example that Thomas cited was Ålandsbanken, a small Finnish bank with around 700 staff:

> They are a local bank and they wanted people to be more aware of their environmental footprint. Many banks ascribe a certain category to the products you buy. So for example if I buy a beer, it would be under 'beverages' and it puts an industry on your actual bank account so you can get a quick

graphical overview of your spending and what categories you spend. What they then did was to add a calculation of your estimated carbon footprint on all those categories. So again they are empowering me to take matters into my own hands and then be able to offset that with various projects in the Baltic region. This makes business sense as it helps people to think about how money is connected to the environment.

Much of Thomas's work is closely aligned with Customer Experiences with Soul, especially the search for authenticity and the maximum coherence between what a person or brand says, what they mean, and what they do. He likes campaigns such as Amex's *Small Business Saturday,* where the brand completely takes a backseat and empowers people and makes them an ambassador of the message:

> I like campaigns which allow people to take matters into their own hands.

Looking to the future, economic inequality is the big issue that Thomas is now aiming to tackle:

> I don't think we can solve the environmental crisis if we do not solve the social crisis. People have such exorbitant wealth – it just doesn't make sense.

It is interesting that every so often representatives from major organisations do get in touch with Thomas asking him not to make public statements about them, or to tone down his criticisms. So we finished our conversation by asking Thomas if he could put into his own words the meaning of 'good':

> For me it is about feeling. I have the most basic definition of it. For me it comes down to gut feeling. This is why I

sometimes have mixed feelings about helping some companies and talking about them. I do bash brands, but that is
because I feel they do a lot of bad stuff so why should I keep
quiet? I don't think you should sell some products, for example, foods targeted at children and which are high in sugar.

Entrepreneur and fund partner Gunther Sonnenfeld, co-founder of
Exile Leadership, also takes a similar view to Thomas. Along with
Andrew Markell, Gunther co-created the Smart Ecologies regenerative economic platform, a framework and platform which provides stable alternatives to evolving business and economic systems.
Gunther says that the task for organisations is "to create assets in the
form of natural resources and to figure out ways to distribute them
into these local markets, teaching people how to use those resources
for the benefit of their community". He makes the point that it is
rare to hear a CEO or president talk about how their business will
transform a whole marketplace. The traditional business mindset sees
people as 'consumers', where the focus is "normally only about how
they are going to innovate and how they are going to do their thing".

One of the underlying assumptions behind the Smart Ecologies
platform is that "economic and ecological scenarios can't just be
tested cognitively, they must be experienced (like reality) and understood emotionally, physically, spiritually and transactionally by
each and every participant".[125] This resonates with our *Holonomics*
approach, which helps people to move beyond intellectual models
and frameworks for change and to shift into a more empathic way of
thinking about the lived experience of each person in an ecosystem.

Gunther's philosophy is one of shifting our thinking away from
only increasing sales and consumption, and instead directing it towards empowering people:

You need to empower people, actually enable their growth
by giving them real utilities and assets which help them in

their daily lives. These can be anything from technology innovations (apps) which measure and redistribute energy usage to open curricula around emerging industries like vertical or urban farming that show people how to grow their own organic food. Over the years we've worked with dozens of companies from startups to multinationals to wealthy family businesses, some of whom have understood this and have fulfilled this approach in smaller ways. They've mostly done this by enabling supply chains, and some have developed joint ventures that significantly improve the environment and create new jobs and new skills areas.

But the real story is what's possible when all the normative mental models are broken down and companies can focus on the actual civic requirements of a market – what people and communities really need in terms of natural, intellectual and creative resources. Civic requirements equate to a total market opportunity that is in the trillions. Here in the United States, all you need to do is travel to cities like Detroit, Topeka and East Camden to see both the devastation and the opportunity for yourself.

Here's the thing: companies historically have never really thought about how closely aligned their operational footprints and addressable market opportunities are, mostly because they segment populations as 'consumers' rather than human beings with socioeconomic attributes and conditions which constantly change. This is the boon in the 'sustainability' or regenerative economy equation.

Brazil is one country in which much positive change is already happening. This change for the good is not just being driven by large organisations, but by communities, towns, villages and often just small groups of people wishing to help their friends, families and neighbours. In January 2011, tired of only hearing bad news, Iara and Eduardo Xavier sold their home and left Divinópolis in Minas Gerais, Brazil with a single goal – to hunt down good stories across the country. Their mission is to find people who make a difference in the community in which they live, running a social project or taking positive action.[126] By May 2016, after 64 months of exploring they had covered 225,000 km cataloguing 1,322 outstanding projects across 18 different states. They do not scour the internet for projects; they simply arrive in cities and towns and get tips from people they meet. They then turn up unannounced, so as to ensure that they experience the projects in as pure a way as possible. As they say on their Facebook page, *Caçadores de Bons Exemplos* (Hunters of Good Examples), which has over 123,000 followers:

> We believe that there are much more positive actions than negative actions in the world. Our goal is to raise awareness in the hope that people will do the same as the good examples we find, and also to encourage people to help those who are already doing this.[127]

Iara and Xavier have four clear objectives:

Change the way of seeing

They wish to show humanity at its very best, that everywhere there are people who are searching for solutions, not just problems, and that there are more positive actions rather than negative actions in the world. They wish to counter the daily news of murder, theft and tragedies by showing who the people are who are building a better world.

Inspire

They wish to inspire more people to become agents of positive change, thus multiplying the impact that they are having.

Connecting

Some people may not wish or may not be able to get involved in ambitious or large-scale projects. Nonetheless, there is still a role to play in helping connect people together, forming a network of those who wish to help others.

Valuing

Their desire is to motivate those who they meet and are already doing good, encouraging them to continue on their path.

Along with the realities of corruption and malpractice many Brazilians are seeking ways in which they can make a difference not only to their own lives, but to the lives of all Brazilians. Thomas Giordano (aged 17) and Pedro Oliveira (aged 18) are two young Brazilians who have had enough of what is often referred to as the *jeitinho brasileiro*, a phrase which can be translated as 'the Brazilian way of doing things'. This phrase often has negative connotations, referring to petty forms of corruption.

Thomas and Pedro decided to set up a new and inspirational initiative *O Novo Jeitinho Brasileiro* ('The New Brazilian Way'). We had an opportunity to speak to them about their project, their manifesto and their dream of a better Brazil. "The *jeitinho brasileiro* has a lot of negative connotations of trying to doing things as fast as possible and not doing things for the good of people around you and your community", explained Pedro. "We believe that most of what is going on in Brazil, in terms of corruption and of misman- agement in government, comes from this culture of people doing things for themselves and not for others. We're trying to change the meaning of the *jeitinho brasileiro*, which is why we are calling it The

New Brazilian Way. We're trying to give a new meaning to the old Brazilian way, which meant doing things for yourself, not caring about others, not caring about future generations, and instead actually doing things for others, and trying to build a better place not just for yourself, but for others, and not trying to do things as fast as possible, but wanting the best results for everybody".

They aim to tell stories about people who are actually doing things in the new Brazilian way, and living their lives without "little acts of corruption" such as small bribes to junior officials, and "simple things such as queue jumping". They call these people "idols" as they are the ones who are trying to change Brazil, "ordinary people who are really setting an example, being ethical and supporting others". Thomas describes their manifesto as "a synthesis of everything we wish to share with our project". It begins with the well-known adage that Brazil has always been "the country of the future" but that it has never managed to reach the population's vision of progress and a better Brazil. So at the heart of the manifesto is the idea that the only way for Brazil to *be* the country of the future is to move to the new Brazilian way. Their great desire is for people to recognise Brazil as a country which is beautiful not just for its nature, but also for the beauty in the affectionate nature of the people too.

A key theme that runs throughout Gadamer's work is that 'the Good' always remains intangible and always out of our reach. In our exploration of beauty we have already seen Gadamer's belief that "the beautiful reveals itself in the search for the good". This is an excellent example of finding beauty in the souls and nature of those who are continually striving to be and do good. Beauty has a transcendental moral and ethical quality, since it forms a bridge between the ideal pictures of life which we would love to be experiencing and the realities of our daily lives. Beauty radiates and lights up our souls, which recognise the good as beautiful.

In April 2016 Caio Rossoni was having a problem with the plug on his smart phone and so he went to Rua Santa Ifigênia, a well-known street in São Paulo where there are a number of technology shops which also carry out minor repairs. He went into an arcade where a number of kiosks are all located side by side. At the first one he went into the staff did not even look at the phone; they simply said to him that it would cost R$180 (around £40) to repair. Cursing to himself at that quote, he decided to see if there was another kiosk which could do the repair. Nearby to the first was another called Rei do Iphone (King of the iPhone) and on showing his phone to Wissam Mohamad, one of the staff, he received the reply that the socket on the phone was dirty. Wissam took out a small tool, gave the phone the once over and returned it to Caio, telling him that it was now fine. "How much is that?", asked Caio, and the owner simply replied, "Nothing. But here is my card. Please can you tell a few friends about my business?"

Caio left the kiosk smiling and happy, with the problem resolved. He posted a photo of the business card onto his Facebook page, praising this small act of honesty. What happened next was quite remarkable. The small kiosk normally received around fifteen clients a day. After Caio uploaded his photo, visits increased to 150 per day, with people asking to replace the glass and batteries on their phones, and seeing what they had in terms of headphones and other accessories. According to Rei do iPhone, their sales increased by 900%, with Caio's post receiving 331,000 likes, 72,756 shares and over 1,000 comments.[128]

Small acts like this, acts which epitomise righteousness, regularly go unnoticed and unsung each day. This little story received attention in Brazil's media for the size and scale of the response to people who, like Caio, were fed up with always being taken advantage of by other repair shops. In the myth of *Phaedrus*, Plato tells of the journey of the soul into the heavens, where it is possible to view the true order of things, writing, "All soul looks after all that lacks a soul, and patrols all of heaven, taking different shapes at different times".[129] But with social media in our modern age, people are striving to search for the good, finding good souls, lighting up our own souls as we recognise the good in these beautiful stories.

Justice

Marketing is no longer about Product, Price, Place and Promotion. The new four Ps are People, Planet, Platforms and Purpose. The new economy is emerging, but for authentic collaboration to take place, there have to be both shared values and shared value. In the new economy people are rethinking the meaning of value, developing new models based on cooperation and collaboration. If we break down the word collaboration, we find three elements:

co – meaning company, as in the company of others.
lab – meaning laboratory, the sense of experimentation.
ration – the etymology from which we can derive 'ratio'.

If we analyse the dynamics of any particular collaboration, especially in the 'new' sharing economy, we need to look at the ratio of the sharing to the outcome as well as the input. A scenario that we have witnessed a number of times is the dynamic of the initiator seeking to exploit the ideas and efforts of others for their own gain. Thus the ratios of the outputs are all geared towards the commander, who always retains full control of the project. It is the old exploitative logic with a new vocabulary.

The situation is also exacerbated by the added element of volunteering. This is an interesting dynamic to explore, since at times the initiator (the person or group seeking volunteers) will have received funding, either through explicit sponsorship or through less obvious means. While therefore receiving some kind of income, the initiator will still expect others to volunteer both their time and resources or intellectual property. Where volunteering is centred around innovation, sharing and volunteering models are open to exploitation, for example, where there are no contracts in place which define how intellectual property can be shared. This is quite a different situation, for example, from open technology standards, since those companies and organisations moving to open standards will have very clear strategic, tactical and well-thought-out business models which make sense commercially.

In this age of non-governmental organisations (NGOs) and not-for-profit organisations where consultants receive payment from corporate sponsors who are looking to create a project based on volunteering, sometimes volunteers feel awkward, uncomfortable and unrewarded. The volunteers may join a collaborative project full of hope and with the desire to improve a social, ecological or political situation, but when the dynamics of knotworks start to bubble up, then the leaders may well encounter turbulence, which can easily lead to recriminations, arguments and sourness. If these issues of predators, ego and knotworks are not acknowledged and dealt with in advance, the project will struggle to remain sustainable and will ultimately run the risk of collapse. If leaders fail to address these shadow aspects of human nature, all the great, uplifting and wonderful exhortations to volunteer and share will come to nothing. Ultimately, the quality of our collaborations depends on a deeper relationship – the nature of our relationship with money.

In 2010, we had the chance to spend the week with Per Espen Stocknes, author of *Money and Soul: The Psychology of Money and the Transformation of Capitalism*. His book is a fascinating journey through the history of money from the perspective of both economics and psyche and how these two concepts have always been opposed throughout humanity, for example, money *or* soul, finance *or* feelings, markets *or* common humanity. Stocknes examines the great question of our spiritual and emotional relationship with money, and asks if we can find a new way of looking at, using and thinking about it, allowing us to develop new ideas of finance for the future.[130] Dysfunctional archetypal behaviour often stems from a fear of missing out, and a fear that others will gain and we will lose. Hence these behaviours often centre around money and our feelings towards those who have it and those who may have a better ability to earn it. The move towards the gig economy, with everyone hustling for contracts and clients, is exacerbating these fears and fights. There is more competition than ever before, but much of it remains hidden and unacknowledged within knotworks and dysfunctional collaborative projects.

When people act from ego, they are not aware of the way in which their words, actions and body language are perceived by others, revealing themselves as counterfeit. 'Counterfeit' in this instance means declaring one objective or purpose for a project or initiative when in fact the true purpose is either deliberately withheld, or hidden down in the subconscious. Because these dynamics are often below the surface, when we are at the stage of putting together a team in a collaborative project we need to take certain precautions. Discernment is a necessary precaution for protection before accepting offers to collaborate, and the one question that we ask – in a gentle and not hostile manner – is where the funds are coming from to support the person who is asking others to collaborate and share. If there is just one person, or a small number of individuals who will benefit financially from a project which is based on the input and involvement of a larger number of other people, then this particular project may not be sustainable in the longer term.

People still do need to earn money in the new economy, and so the concept of volunteering and 'sharing' has to be understood, or otherwise we will just have a more distorted economy benefitting the few project leaders and platform owners who receive income, adulation and credit at the expense of a larger silent and invisible majority. If a person is operating not from ego but from a deep position of lived human values, then they will understand the need to ask this question about the source of their funding. In order to ask this question, you need to have your own understanding and relationship with money fully worked out. Our relationship with money needs to be soulful. If all parties concerned have a shared set of values, then the next step should be in agreeing a contract, even if only a brief document which outlines the expectations and responsibilities of everyone concerned. Even when the collaboration is one of volunteering, a contract represents the embodiment of shared values and is an important part of the process of developing a joint understanding of the project or venture under consideration. Contracts do not need to involve lawyers; they can be simple written agreements. The lack of any documented agreements can cause problems further down the line if problems arise and there is disagreement and no shared understanding.

While we are witnessing major technical developments in relation to electronic money, we need to be mindful of the need to develop our psychological and spiritual relationships around money. If those who are asking others to give up their valuable free time and contribute ideas and intellectual property that have taken years to form and evolve, are not able to be transparent in their business models and sources of funding, then you need to be cautious before deciding to make a commitment. In any collaboration which is fair and just, there is a shared sense of values. It is therefore interesting to explore justice in organisations by studying their value propositions. Value propositions often mean different things to different people, but if we view them through the lens of justice, we can see them as tools of alignment, aligning what is good for the business with what is good for the customer. Value propositions are not mere statements of what a company does; they are the value experience which is delivered. Thus, value is created in the ecosystem.[131]

There are three different approaches to value creation. The first is the inside-out approach, where the attitude of the business is "Here's our offering. Take it or leave it". The second is outside-in, where the attitude of the customer is "I want what I want. If it bankrupts you that's your problem". Neither of these approaches is sustainable in the long term. The third approach, taken by Cindy Barnes, Helen Blake and David Pinder in their book *Creating and Delivering Your Value Proposition: Managing Customer Experience for Profit,* is the value-focused approach (Figure 11). A key insight from their work is that a value proposition is not what you do; it is the value experience which you deliver. As they point out, before you can step into another's shoes, you have to take off your own. Therefore we end up with the conclusion that the real power of value proposition thinking is in the process.

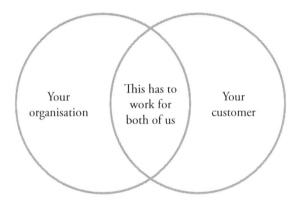

Figure 11: The Value-Focused Approach

Helen Blake is the Chief Executive of Futurecurve, a company which is helping businesses to achieve truly customer-centric focus. Futurecurve define customer-centricity as "the continuous and active involvement of the customer throughout the whole organisation in the co-design, provision and use of desirable products and services for mutual benefit". Futurecurve are helping leaders in organisations to develop holonomic thinking, and one way in which they are doing so is by using the powerful but rarely used technique called Interpretive Phenomenological Analysis.[132] Helen explained the benefits to us in the following way:

My experience in helping organisations around the world build total value propositions shows how vital it is to include the real feelings and experiences of customers, especially in a world where the balance of power is shifting toward the customer. Yet it is remarkable how hard it is for the customer's voice to be heard inside an organisation. I have seen a proliferation in the use of tools and metrics around customer experience, yet these tools very often serve to reinforce internal mantras and beliefs about what customers want. The end result is that genuine feelings and wants of customers are dissipated and filtered out by the very metrics designed to measure them. Organisations spend so much time, so much effort in creating mechanistic processes for dealing with the customer. Wouldn't it be wonderful if the balance were redressed to include the genuine, holistic feelings and experiences of value from that same customer? Holonomic thinking offers us a fascinating way forward for redressing the balance, so that the organisation and the customer experience something of equal value.

Many concepts relating to value propositions are often discussed in a Cartesian manner, meaning that both the customer experience itself and the processes of developing customer value become codified. The holonomic circle provides a radical new way to think about value propositions by helping designers, marketeers and entrepreneurs go 'upstream' into the act of seeing itself, where you enter into the lived experience of others. The customer experience is no longer merely quantified using traditional measures, but also described by mapping its qualities, because it also includes each and every person in an ecosystem developing a shared understanding of mutual value, and hence of justice.

It takes wisdom to be able to reflect on who you are, what your brand is, and the relationship between your own identity and the brand identity. Wisdom is continually required to contemplate the way in which reality manifests itself through language, for language is the way in which reality becomes intelligible. Great business leaders are great conversationalists, characterised by their ability to converse and connect with every single person in their organisation and ecosystem, always being aware of how language can both disclose reality to us. They are alert to the way in which language can also conceal reality to us if we get stuck in one particular mindset, such as limiting ourselves to conversations with senior directors, executives and institutional investors.

Plato's Ideas included being and non-being, unity (or the One) and difference (the many), 'motion', 'rest', truth, beauty and goodness. These Ideas are all internally related to one another, and together they are seen as what is common to all Being. Being, the final transcendental, and the dynamics of being, are the subject of the next chapter.

7. The Dynamics of Being

Wholeness in Lived Experience

We are now on the cusp of a shift into a new paradigm in which companies are able to authentically co-create experiences with their customers. Those who will be truly disruptive will be the ones who have mastered the question of being, and who have an ability to co-create on the basis of the lived experience of their customers, rather than on models of the customer experience couched in a fragmented subject/object dichotomy. These are companies who have a wiser, expanded level of awareness which comes from a more primary way of knowing the world.

Our normal way of thinking focuses on objects, namely *what* has been experienced, rather than moving back upstream into the *experiencing* of what is experienced.[133] The greatest lesson which Henri Bortoft taught Simon is that our experience of reality is already whole. In order to understand the wholeness of lived experience we do not start with our present Cartesian representation of reality, which is a universe consisting of discrete elements. We also do not start by thinking of discrete systems which are nested in greater systems:

> People try to make wholeness happen, but it is already there, it is ubiquitous. If you try and impose wholeness, all you do is introduce counterfeit wholeness on top of the wholeness which is already there. No one sees this because they do not

understand the dynamics of the whole and the part. We have an amazing ability for abstract thought, which allows us to live amazing lives. But it produces separation and abstracts from the whole. It gives the illusion of separate autonomous existences. No one thinks about this in full awareness. We believe that there are separate objects, and then worry that the world has fragmented. But we have not seen that things are already related.

This has been said in many contexts. A thing only has its existence as a network of relationships, and it is the relationships which are primary. But we think of the world as separate building blocks and wonder how to put it together. Physics has had to give up this idea in quantum physics. The question we really need to ask ourselves is "how does it come about that things seem to be separate when they are not?" It is the origin of separation that is the problem, not wholeness because the wholeness is already there. Lived experience is holistic. We describe lived experience just a tiny moment after it has been lived. In the actual living experience then you find that it is already holistic. It breaks apart when it becomes experience that has been lived. Then we try and put it together again to make a whole, but we end up creating a counterfeit whole.[134]

Something is clearly getting in the way of our ability to see and perceive the wholeness in experience which is already ubiquitous. People are searching for wholeness when it is already there. If we stick to traditional methods of describing the customer experience, we end up with an objectified description of experience. We need to be able to make the subtle shift into the experience of *what* is experienced, the *seeing* of what is seen, or the saying of what is said. We need to be able to shift our attention into the place where the world appears.

In the later part of his life, Heidegger became increasingly concerned that metaphysics inevitably leads to nihilism and what he called "the forgetfulness of Being".[135] When we talk about 'being', we are referring to a discussion about a 'what' and a 'this'. When we experience something, we always try to relate one particular thing to a more general 'what' and so in an attempt to interpret our experience our thinking continually moves back and forth between the particular thing and the more general concept.[136] We can therefore think of 'being' as a movement rather than a static idea, and in doing so we can think of the transcendentals not as discrete beings or things or even ideas of things but as "principles which determine everything that *is*".[137]

When we explore Being, what something is in its essence, we are always confronted with the problem that Being is at one and the same time both "one and many" or "identity in difference". Through actively contemplating every component of the holonomic circle, we are able to develop a dynamic understanding of who we are, what our brand is, and the relationship between our own identity and our brand identity. When we focus not only on the appearance of things, but also on the appear*ance* (the coming-into-being, the happening of the appearing), we end up replacing a two-world theory where appearance and being are separate, and instead we arrive at the dynamics of being.[138]

We are constantly creating new products, services, brands and experiences, and yet few companies explore 'being' at this level of analysis. In his book *Taking Appearance Seriously*, Henri Bortoft addresses two hermeneutical questions: the question of unfinished meaning, and the question of multiple meaning[139]. In relation to a written text, the common sense way of thinking about how we understand what someone has written is to create a division between what the author had in mind and the subjective understanding in the reader's mind. However, this creates a number of immediate problems, namely that we cannot jump into the mind of the reader and check that it is an exact reproduction of the original meaning. Given that readers understand the same text differently, how are we to know which of these interpretations is the 'correct' one? Hermeneutics does not objectify meaning into units of data to be analysed computationally, but instead takes our thinking 'upstream' into the 'happening of meaning', a phrase Henri used to alert us to the appearance of meaning, that point where meaning appears. When you are in an upstream mode of consciousness, 'meaning' is not separated from 'understanding', there is in fact a unitary act of meaning/understanding:

> The meaning does not appear first, and then we understand it. Understanding is not a response to a meaning which is there already; it is the appearance of meaning. So we can say that the appearance of meaning is the happening of understanding.[140]

There is a switch of perspective in which the subject is not now seen as the interpreter but instead as a recipient in which the meaning appears. When we make this switch in perspective, we need to maintain the dynamic relationship between the One and the many, as we have seen in the example of Hamlet (chapter six). Meaning is neither one of free interpretation open to any subjective whim, but nor is it dogmatically closed or ultimately definable. At one and the same time there is always the One play, the One text and the One brand, as well as there also being many Hamlets, and thus many true interpretations and many experiences of brands.

Gadamer discussed 'unfinished meaning', drawing our attention to the fact that we can never arrive at an ultimate meaning of something that we have created; there is always room for the meaning of something, the being, to expand.[141] The being of something can increase. One way in which we can explore this notion of being and meaning is through play. When we are at play, we have the option of exploring many different possibilities, allowing us to develop our awareness and understanding of who we are. Games therefore help us to contemplate being, and one way in which play can be introduced into organisations is through experiential learning interventions using the Holonomics approach, which we shall now explore.

Calor Humano

Every single person in an organisation has a role to play in delivering a customer experience with soul, starting with those at the very top and the stories they chose to tell. Stories show the relationships and connections between people and explain why things happen. By developing experiential games with clear narratives, it is possible to create stories which help people to make sense of what the organisation is trying to achieve, regardless of their background, education or experience.

One organisation which utilised the holonomics approach to storytelling was Hospital Sírio Libanês, one of the most important hospitals in Brazil and South America, located in the central Bela Vista district of São Paulo. In addition to the Bela Vista complex, the hospital has five complementary units: one diagnostic centre and day hospital in Itaim Bibi, São Paulo; a unit in Jardins, also in São Paulo; and two oncology units and one diagnostic centre in Brasília. Dr. Paulo Chapchap is the CEO of the hospital, and we spoke to him about the hospital, why it manages to achieve such a high quality of healthcare, and the impact of introducing holonomic thinking into their strategy and communication programmes.

The first time Dr. Chapchap worked at the hospital was as an apprentice in his fifth year at medical school. He began to specialise in child surgery and paediatrics, followed by studying for a fellowship in Pittsburgh, USA for two years. On his return he created the procedures for some of the first liver transplant operations in

Brazil. At the hospital he became a paediatric surgeon in addition to carrying out liver transplants. Hospital Sírio Libanês is a not-for-profit organisation, founded in 1921 by a group of women who came from the Middle East. Wanting to give back to Brazilian society the welcome that their families received, they decided that there was no better way of doing so than to create a hospital which was open to all social classes. This is still the strongest sentiment that everyone has at the hospital:

> We recognise we are a society with huge inequality and that it is we who are the ones who are lucky. The thing that determines success in Brazilian society is still your family, where you were born. This is still the strongest driver of your comfort and security. You can move from class to class, but it is not easy to do this. If our lives have privilege we have to give it back to society to decrease the inequality. This is the strongest sentiment we have here.

It is interesting to think about the moral and ethical dimensions of leadership in the context of a hospital, since, as Dr. Chapchap says, "It is not morally defensible to have a competitive advantage in healthcare". While the hospital constantly searches for excellence, they also look to share their knowledge:

> If you know something that can make a difference for the patient, you can't keep it for yourself. You have to spread it out so that everyone can develop it together. Leadership here means sharing knowledge, sharing strategy and sharing values. And it also means trying to develop the whole system instead of seeing your institution in a competitive way compared to other institutions. Of course you want to be the first to do things, of course you want to do things in the best way possible. Once you find a better way, you have

to spread the news. You have to publish it. That is why I am always enthusiastic about spreading the news and the ways in which you are doing things. This is very important.

Dr. Chapchap is acutely aware of the role and impact which the senior leadership team have in relation to the customer experience:

I do not believe you can create a good environment for people who are fragile if you are very competitive inside your institution. I think that if you create such a competitive environment you will lose your capacity to lead with the warmth, sensitivity and human values. I believe that you can seek results via relationships and not on competitiveness. There are, therefore, two drivers of collaboration. Firstly, being a leader is about sharing knowledge and the ways you do things. Secondly, it is about creating a collaborative environment, and not a competitive environment. These are the key things about leadership and healthcare.

Hospital Sírio Libanês is also a teaching hospital, offering post-graduate and residential courses. Medical students come to the hospital from across Brazil to study, and distance-learning courses are also available. Their growth strategy is based on education, personal development, and opening other units in this São Paulo and around Brazil. The values of the hospital are Pioneering, Social Responsibility, Knowledge, Excellence and *Calor Humano*, a term which can be translated as 'human warmth', a concept which we will be examining shortly. If we start to look at Hospital Sírio Libanês through the framework of the holonomic circle, starting with the trinity, they are an excellent example of an organisation for which 'What I say', 'What I do' and 'What I mean' are all highly coherent (as described in chapter two). An example is seen in the way in which Dr. Chapchap describes their strategy:

Since we designed the strategy to attract, retain and develop good people, we think we are above average in the Brazilian market. Of course we do want to grow. Our aim is to occupy positions that other institutions which are not as dedicated to the patient as we are, cannot to reach, thereby developing the system. But if we only do this, we are going to be competing for market share. The way we wish to grow without competing is via education. Here we also train people in the public system because we know that we will be developing and improving the whole system. The public system really needs this training.

For some years the senior team at the hospital had been developing their business strategy and their strategic map, which included people, sustainability and philanthropy as major pillars. The challenge which they then faced was how to communicate this strategic map to the entire hospital, to every single person at every single level. Together with the strategy, marketing and HR teams at the hospital, Simon was asked to help develop a communications event to enable them to do this, and the solution was based on the philosophy of wholeness of *Holonomics*. The overall objective was to communicate the new strategy to all 4,500 members of staff. These staff worked at all levels in the organisation, and the communication would not be limited to certain levels of management. Because of the nature of their work, no single individual could be away from their positions for more than one hour.

Having clarified these two elements, the challenge was to think about 'meaning' and 'relationships' (from Tools and Techniques in the holonomic circle), and how these aspects would inform the design. In order to create a compelling educational experience which engaged people emotionally and which would bring people together to develop a sense of being one team, both the the corporate culture and national social dynamics would need to be taken into account.

Brazil is a country with major inequality, and this has resulted in a society where the distances between social classes (not just between the very top and the very bottom) are far greater than more equal societies such as Sweden or the United Kingdom. The design brief was to create an event which brought together people from every level of the hospital – porters, security staff, janitors, secretaries, receptionists, nurses, nutritionists, managers, doctors, executives, directors and surgeons. For the design to take into account social dynamics, sensitivity would be needed to the differing lived experiences of each person, anticipating who would understand the concept of a strategic map, and who would potentially feel alienated, confused or simply unable to relate to a technical and unfamiliar tool.

Every minute of this experience would have to be maximised, and so the actual experience started as soon as people arrived at the reception area where the sessions were being held. Over the course of one week one-hour sessions were run with up to 100 people each, training 2,500 people in total. People registered their attendance, and then in order to enter the main room they walked through a curtain into a 'time tunnel' which was a short corridor telling the story of the hospital from its founding in 1921 to the present day. As they did so, they began to connect with the soul of the hospital. Every detail of the experience of each participant had been carefully through, including the use of dramatic and cinematic music which filled everyone with excited expectation of what was to come.

The participants were able to choose where to sit at one of ten tables, which each had up to ten people. Through gentle guidance, each table ended up with a wide mix of collaborators from every area and department in the hospital. Each table could be thought of as a hologram of Hospital Sírio Libanês, whereby the essence of the hospital was being expressed through each group as a whole and also through every person. Every table contained the strategic map told as a story, stretching from one end to the other. Each story was therefore so long that one person could only read a part. The result was that doctors and surgeons listened to secretaries and nutritionists tell the story of how the hospital aimed to be positioned in 2020, and so this was a way to melt the social hierarchy almost without people noticing, moving away from hierarchical social dynamics and towards an experience of wholeness.

It was interesting for us to observe Dr. Chapchap during the sessions which he attended. For the vast majority of the time, when walking around, he listening rather than speaking. Not only did he listen, but he also totally trusted in the process, not imposing his thoughts on others, but allowing every participant to express themselves. Very few senior executives of his level have his humility, presence, and ability to really see each and every individual in the whole organisation. His presence and manner contrasted quite markedly with one very senior executive, who did not sit down at a table with the rest of the team, but who chose to remain standing. This executive ignored the instructions given and decided to interpret the story in their own way, and rather read a part of the carefully worded narrative, they told the whole table what it all meant in their own vocabulary. The body language of many participants on this table were completely different from the others, the seniority and dominance of this particular executive being very apparent. This table lost a huge opportunity in the initial stages to start to gel as non-hierarchical team, and the energy was also palpably lower. When we do not take into account the lived experience of others, then no matter what position we hold in an organisation, people react to our personal customer experience, meaning that we miss important opportunities to develop as a team and achieve great results collectively.

We asked people to create a picture, model or story that embodied the solutions which they had put forward. A key phrase which came up time and again was *calor humano,* one of the core values of the hospital, and which is the sense of friendliness, empathy and care that every member of staff has with each patient and guest of the hospital. We can think of *calor humano* as the strategic map as it comes to presence in each and every member of Hospital Sírio Libanês. One young employee drew 'the sandals of humility', in reference to a Brazilian comedy show with a recurring sketch where comedians would chase glamorous celebrities and ask them to take off their shoes and wear the golden sandals of humility, to show that they were not arrogant and had not lost touch with reality. This employee told everyone present that sometimes he wished that those who were at the most senior levels could sometimes wear the sandals of humility and recognise the contributions of his own peer group a little more. His drawing of the sandals of humility was a very cogent visual metaphor and it was wonderful to listen to him talk about how his great wish for more significant and meaningful integration across collaborators.

Designing interventions such as this by using the holonomic circle and the philosophy of *Holonomics* can be extremely powerful, due to the way in which people become engaged in issues and problems in an entirely different manner from business as usual. We spoke to Dr. Chapchap after the sessions so as to gain an understanding of how effective this particular intervention had been. It was interesting to hear Dr. Chapchap explain why the senior executive team had felt the need to communicate the strategy to each and every person at the hospital. He also outlined his own personal philosophy of leadership, and what the implications were for the customer experience of patients:

> Communicating the strategy is fundamental. There is a huge difference between designing a strategy and implementing it. They are different worlds. We don't think we can do this without the collaboration of all people who work here. They have to understand, they have to get involved, and they have to help us execute and modify it if that is what is needed. You saw that. People were suggesting new things all the time.

For an institution to have sustainable growth, it has to develop leaders. But then who exactly is the leader? There was a game – Brazil vs. Italy in 1970 – the final of the World Cup. The final goal was scored by Brazil. It was 4 – 1. In the build up to this goal, six or seven Brazilians touched the ball before it went in and they scored. Everybody did something different. They didn't just receive the ball and pass it. Everyone was planning at that moment they had the ball. That's a very powerful metaphor. The leader is the one who has the ball. So the lesson is that the leader can be anyone in an institution.

If someone goes into a room to clean the floor, and the patient sees that they are doing a good job and talks to them and they reply appropriately, that person is the leader of the healthcare at that time, because he or she is doing a good job in cleaning, interacting with the patient, being warm, knowing what to say. And if the patient complains about something, anything, if they go out and tell the nurse to correct what is wrong, they are the leader of the process at that time. There is no way you can run strategy and develop leaders for the strategy and execution if you don't involve everybody in the strategy. You are going to have a smaller institution.

We asked Dr. Chapchap about his reactions to certain aspects of the event, including the picture of the sandals of humility:

I would differentiate 'modesty' from 'humility'. Modesty in some senses can be a false thing. Real humility is when you know that you don't know everything. You know that other people can teach you. You are still learning and will always be learning from your experiences and so you are open to other people and other knowledge.

Dr Chapchap emphasised the point that the vast majority of surgeons and doctors at the hospital treated others with great respect; he was only talking about a tiny minority of people. All staff are told that if they do speak to a doctor about the way in which they are being treated, they will never be fired. The guidelines are that although no one has to accept disrespect from a doctor, they do have to raise the issue in the right manner, not in front of patients or visitors, but in private.

> *The Sandals of Humility* comes from the phrase *de salto alto,* an expression which means 'stuck up' (on high heels). You are superior. By contrast, the sandals do not have heels – they are flat. That is a very strong image, demonstrating how everyone has to know that they do not know everything. Knowing this makes you do things more carefully. Among people there is a huge variation. If you are conceited or too self-confident, you are going to do things incorrectly. You have to adapt to different needs and different situations, and always learn from the experience. What our collaborators at the hospital say here is that some doctors should wear the sandals of humility, because they think they are gods, but they are not. That is something which has to be said in a hospital, or in any institution where you have a dominating profession.

It was interesting to hear Dr. Chapchap discuss from his perspective what he had learnt at the sessions which he had attended:

> I was learning. There are not many situations where I can meet all the people who work with us – not *for* us, but *with* us – and get a feeling of what they think, what they say, what they are worried about. How can they co-operate and do the things they are doing? That was a wonderful opportunity for

someone in my position, to live together with people and learn. In Portuguese we use the term *conviver*. I was listening because I was learning.

I learned how powerful people can be. Never forget how powerful people can be, no matter what situation they are in. They have their lives, their dreams, their missions. Another way to define an institution which grows sustainably is by its ability to form leaders. Here is the place where people have the means and the tools to develop the mission they have in life, together with the mission they have with their families. Institutions should not substitute for families. Everything is a part of life. They will be better parents if they have a better environment in which to work.

Hospital Sírio Libanês works hard to recruit people who will fit in with their culture, particularly people who live and breathe *calor humano*:

Calor humano is one of our values. It means noticing other people and liking other people. Tolerance is not powerful enough. To tolerate difference is the same as saying you are different, I don't like you but I tolerate you. You have to go beyond tolerance. You have to like diversity. *Calor humano* means looking at a person who you don't know, who you have never met, and still showing that you care. That is *calor humano*. You care for the other person, even though you don't know them yet. You care because you care for humanity.

Caring for your family, siblings, mother and father, that's natural. People have to do more than what is natural. We are not animals. We have to transform ourselves to welcome diversity in people. Being able to show it in the very first moment when you meet someone who is fragile, suffering and afraid, showing that you care, looking into their eyes, using your hands, that is *calor humano.*

It has to be everyone. If you are afraid that you may die, if you are suffering and you are in pain, then every moment that someone looks at you, you will value. If the person is distant, you may think that you are in a bad way. You may think that you are going to die. You can't stand over someone because then you are showing a difference. You have to sit down with a person and look into their eyes.

In relation to communicating the strategy using gamification and the principles of wholeness in *Holonomics*, Dr. Chapchap told us that from now on the hospital was only going to run this kind of programme, process and event using holonomic thinking, and that they would not be returning to the traditional way of doing things:

I told my team more than once that I want to do more of this. Find excuses to do this, reasons to do it. It doesn't matter. We have to do it more often because it is a way for people to live together through a process. Learning the importance of the other and of the importance of diversity, people will come to like other people more, and that makes a better institution. There are other ways you can execute your strategy. But it is the process, the getting people to execute the strategy, the means, which are as important as the end results in this case. This is an example of a means that was very powerful for the strategy.

I believe that we don't play enough. Because of these events people are now starting to understand why I am always in a good mood. You have to create a good environment to do a good job. Your proposal to create this type of event, involving everyone, meant that everyone was creating something. You gave them the responsibility to innovate, to create and communicate what came from inside them. They were playing. It was so right, and on the other hand, it was so productive, light, a good environment, everyone happy, very productive. These are not incompatible. I loved it.

Introducing *Holonomics* into organisations can therefore have a powerful impact due to the way in which people become engaged in issues and problems in an entirely different manner from business as usual. This event was powerful for Hospital Sírio Libanês because, unlike traditional one-way corporate presentations, it was structured to help people come to an understanding of the meaning of the strategy on their own terms, and it gave senior leaders a chance to listen and learn. It created a space for conversations about *calor humano* to emerge, and so here we see how great leaders always look to find ways to help everyone in the organisation to contemplate being, that which expresses the very heart and soul of who they are.

Being and Soul

Philosophers, designers and marketeers all seek to understand how people engage with objects in the world, be they works of art, tools, products or brands. They ask questions so as to understand how people make sense of the world and what, if anything, gives meaning to our lives.[142] Philosophy has the power to make great contributions to our understanding of people, of meaning, of how things in the world can both appear to us and be concealed from us. Heidegger dedicated his life to the understanding of being, and in order to articulate his philosophy he would create his own language for doing so. In an interview about his own philosophy, Gadamer once said that he tried to avoid Heidegger's terminology, saying that Heidegger himself wished that his students would find their own words, and rather than imitate him they should simply be inspired by him.[143]

One of the greatest articulations of Heidegger's philosophy can be found in Tao Ruspoli's documentary film *Being in the World*. More than just an exploration of Heidegger's concept of being, it is also a celebration of humanity, blending commentary from philosophers with interviews from extraordinary people who have achieved mastery across a broad range of activities such as flamenco, jazz, cookery, carpentry, juggling and speed boat racing. This allowed Ruspoli to explore the hypothesis that the most important thing which characterises humans is not the ability to sit back and think rationally and logically about situations; rather, it is our ability to become involved in the world, and our ability to develop skills for acting in those worlds which do not necessarily require intellectual skills but instead involve practical skills. Achieving mastery in a craft is to move from a level of proficiency where we are dependent on following rules to a level of proficiency that is uniquely attuned to the sacred. This is because when we achieve mastery we have the capacity to open up whole new worlds:

> Things only show themselves when all the conditions of skill and all the relationships between them are possible. And then the experience is of something opening up, of possibilities, a way of inhabiting the world opens up, and it's not like it was there all along. Worlds are whole, organised, coherent ways of being human in activities.[144]

One approach to the study of history is to view it in relation to major changes in *worlds*.[145] Throughout history we find that there are fundamentally different conceptions of *being*, or *isness*, our way of understanding what it means for anything to be anything at all.

The earliest period of classical antiquity, the Archaic period, ran from the eighth century BC to the sixth century BC, during which era the early Greek epoch emerged. The name which the ancient Greeks gave to *being* was *physis,* meaning nature. Within this notion of *to be* there were no dynamical aspects such as opening up, blossoming, emergence, birth and decay. In the later Classical Greek epoch we find the term *poïesis* which is generally understood to mean 'making'. It also has a sense of 'revealing' or 'bringing things out'. So, for example, we can say that cooks bring out what is best in the food, and this brings out what is best in the people eating that food.

The Roman sense of *being* was characterised by the imposition of form on matter. Order is imposed on from without. So, for example, instead of bringing things out, like a carpenter with wood, the focus is on hammering things into shape. In the Christian world which followed, we see a subsequent shift to a world view with one single god, a god who is the sole producer and who imposes all the forms on everything. Within this overarching eternal order everything and everyone has their proper place in the hierarchy. While this social, religious and philosophical world view in some ways enabled people to find meaning in their lives, it also meant huge restrictions, limits to personal freedom and authoritarian governing regimes.[146]

The Modern Age ran from the sixteenth century to the twentieth century in which people began to see themselves as giving everything meaning, rather than God. This period also coincides with a new-found focus on measurement. The British Science Museum has a remarkable exhibition titled *Making the Modern World,* which is a huge showcase of the development of technology from the last 250 years. Along with major exhibits such as Stephenson's Rocket, it divides this period into nine key areas:

Enlightenment and Measurement, 1750 – 1820
Manufacture by Machine, 1800 – 1860
The Industrial Town, 1820 – 1880

The Age of the Engineer, 1820 – 1880
The Second Industrial Revolution, 1870 – 1914
The Age of the Mass, 1914 – 1938
Defiant Modernism, 1930 – 1968
Design Diversity, 1950 – 1965
The Age of Ambivalence, 1960 – 2000

Economic development in the early part of the nineteenth century was driving the desire for ever more accurate measurements, weights and standards leading to a new family of scientific instruments (Figure 12). Industries located overseas and the British military required more accurate astronomical tables, more practical methods for finding new colonies, and more accurate methods for mapping them.[147] London became one of the major centres for the development and manufacture of elegant and ever more practical measuring devices.

Figure 12: The Age of Measurement, British Science Museum

An interesting bifurcation took place during the Age of the Engineer, since at the start of this era it was still possible for individual engineers to become superstars, their inventions such as steam trains and viaducts being highly visible to the public. But by the end of this period major projects had grown to a level of complexity which was beyond an individual's ability to grasp:

> Whereas the first industrial revolution was based on coal, steam and iron, the second industrial revolution saw a leap in the complexity of technology and materials. Life at home and at work became transformed by the transmission of electricity, and this era also saw the invention of synthetic dyes, chemical fertilisers, plastics, textiles and new drugs such as aspirin.[148]

Making the Modern World reminds us that the move into mass production led many people at the time to question whether the modernising economies were becoming too machine-like. Would science perfect warfare, or would it contribute to the solving of societal problems? In period after the second world war there was a huge amount of creative design effort to produce low-cost solutions for austere economic conditions. Towards the end of the twentieth century people had ambivalent feelings towards technology, not knowing if it would be a force for good or for worse, for instance advances in biological engineering and the emergence of the surveillance state. The question of what it means to be human in a technological world is now more pertinent than ever before. While today's technology is introducing us to new ways of experiencing the world through mass connectivity and interactions, mass production has led to an obsession with efficiency, seeing everything – including people – as resources which must be optimised. As Hubert Dreyfus has remarked:

The challenge is how to respect technology and use it to get rid of all the dumb stuff we used to have to do, and yet not let it get rid of what matters, and what is local, and what is unique, and what is significant and meaningful for us.[149]

It is interesting to contrast the unquestioning obsession with technological optimisation in business communities with the world of the flamenco master:

Flamenco artists have a deep aversion to being recorded as they have an intuitive sense that recording them and making their performance reproducible in all sorts of foreign contexts is distorting what flamenco is all about.[150]

Spaniard Manuel Molina was a flamenco guitarist with seven best-selling albums, and whose music appeared in a number of films. He describes flamenco poetically:

Flamenco is not classical, flamenco is of the street. It's not mechanical, flamenco is laughter and tears at the same time. It's a way of feeling, of explaining what's happening to you, mediated by music. I sing to life, to the birds and to nature, and to love, caresses and kisses. We have to try and not be seduced by technology, but keep the drive alive to be humans. When a table is handmade, the food which is eaten off it tastes different.[151]

A craftsperson such as a carpenter dedicates their life to learning how to work with wood, and the level of mastery is reached when they start to see things that people without those skills are unable to see. They become someone who inhabits a *world* differently:

When we finally understand mastery, and a responsiveness to the richness of the call to living in the world, then we come to understand that the source of meaning in our lives isn't in us, that's the Cartesian tradition, and it isn't in some supreme being, but it's in our way of being in the world. Being in the world is a unifying phenomenon. When people are at their best and most absorbed in doing a skilful thing, they lose themselves into their absorption, and the distinction between the master and the world disappears.[152]

The most disruptive word you can use in innovation is 'soul'. A customer experience with soul is a sacred experience which honours what it is to be human in our world. Entrepreneurs of the future will be those who disclose new ways of being in the world, which reconnect us to the sacred.

8. Arriving Full Circle

Journeying Through the Holonomic Circle

We started this book by asking the question 'What do we mean by soul?' The reason for doing so was that customer experiences with soul understand people first and foremost as human beings, not as opportunities to make money. While of course there are many well-established techniques such as customer journey mapping for designing customer experiences, we wanted to explore customer experience from the point of view of wholeness, universal human values and 'being', the deepest sense and experience of what it means to be human. We created the holonomic circle in order to introduce deeper conversations around these themes, which for a number of reasons are still only discussed in a few organisational cultures.

In addition to methodologies and techniques for designing customer experiences, new technologies such as virtual reality, algorithms and artificial intelligence are now becoming commercially viable in an attempt to enhance the interactions that we have with businesses. In our book we have focused on 'being' in customer experiences because this is the one aspect of humanity that no artificial intelligence or robot has managed to reach. Scientific knowledge has reached a stage where transhumanism (the merging of human bodies with computer technology) is now a reality, and where we are now able to create bioengineered, genetically-enhanced human beings, in fact entirely new species of humans. We are the first species on our planet to have the ability to consciously evolve our bodies.

Wherever the primary motivation for developing new technologies is profit, growth, power, domination or a combination of these factors, there is little time for the contemplation of being and soul. But as we have seen, there are inspirational entrepreneurs and business leaders who are driven by higher visions and an enlightened approach to the design and delivery of their products and services, resulting in customer experiences with soul. So, for example, the essence of Laces and Hair is an understanding and sense of beauty which values inner beauty and well-being above all. Chaordic Systems show us that no matter how hi tech a company can be, there is always a place for love. Eduardo Srur shows us that within large corporations there are people who understand the power of art to transform our consciousness and to teach us that big businesses can play an important part in solving social and ecological problems. The New Brazilian Way project reminds us that our concept of customer experience extends to the daily experience that others have of ourselves, and that small acts of kindness can combine together to transform whole societies. And the case study of Hospital Sírio Libanês shows us just how much an organisation can achieve when every single person is valued and when an executive team is able to develop a sensitivity to the lived experience of each individual, no matter where their place in the organisation and society may be.

This final chapter is dedicated to our final in-depth case study of Famiglia Mancini, which we first discussed in the section on Identity and Difference in chapter six. In November 2016 we were able to spend the morning speaking to Walter Mancini at his flagship restaurant Il Ristaurante, who shared with us his story, his approach to business and his philosophy, which for us encapsulates in its entirety our Customer Experiences with Soul framework (Figure 13).

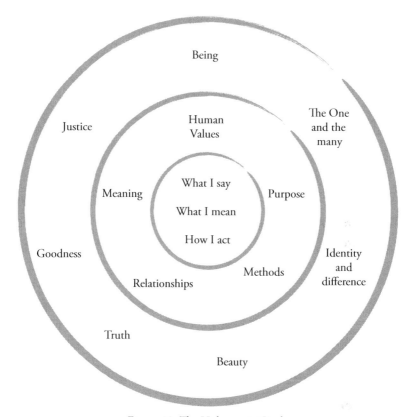

Figure 13: The Holonomic Circle

It is important to note that the circular lines of the holonomic circle are not closed, but remain open, drawing our attention to the way in which the elements of the circle are not to be thought of as separately existing objects or ideas, but rather as fully interrelated. The openness expresses movement, and this is how you can work with the holonomic circle, taking each element as inspiration for dialogues to explore and collectively understand customers, their experiences and the meaning of brands.

The design of the circles were chosen for their likeness to an *ensō*, a hand-drawn symbol from Zen Buddhism expressing a moment when the mind is free to let the body create. According to Audrey

Yoshiko Seo, author of *Ensō: Zen Circles of Enlightenment*, "Zen circles, ensō, are symbols of teaching, reality, enlightenment, and a myriad of things in between. Seemingly perfect in their continuity, balance, and sense of completeness, and yet often irregular in execution, ensō are at once the most fundamentally simple and the most complex shape. They seem to leave little room for variation, and yet in the hands of Zen masters, the varieties of personal expression are endless".[153]

You are about to read an extended interview with Walter Mancini. This was without a doubt one of the most uplifting and beautiful interviews that we ever have recorded, leaving us with a sensation that we had been in the presence of a true master, a soul who is fully in touch with his own sense of being and who has that rare ability to fully connect with the souls of others. As you read the interview, you will see that Walter touches on every single aspect of the holonomic circle, and that he and Famiglia Mancini fully embody the knowledge, understanding and spirit of a business run according to holonomic principles.

Love, Beauty, Generosity and Soul

A little over seventy years ago, Walter Mancini was born close to the municipal market in São Paulo. Known by locals simply as Mercadão ('Big Market'), the market was inaugurated on 25th January, 1933 as a wholesale and retail post specialising in fruits, vegetables, cereals, meats, spices and other food products. It is open to the public and it is one of the main touristic attractions in the city. The structure, built in an eclectic style between 1928 and 1933, is noted for its columns, vaults and stained glass. It occupies an area of 12,600 square metres, employs more than 1,600 people and who together handle about 600 tons of food per day in its more than 300 booths.[154] When listening to Walter, it was clear just how much influence his formative years in this abundant culinary microcosm had had on his outlook on life, cuisine and understanding of people.

One of the most remarkable aspects of Walter as a person is his poetical way of speaking. From the start of our conversation to the very end, his speech is full of heart, full of feeling, articulated in Portuguese which is naturally a far more lyrical language than English, which is much more technical in its nature. In our translations, therefore, we have worked hard to capture his enchanting way of speaking, such as keeping the word 'creatures' which Walter uses when he refers to people, including himself. It is the same sense that is found in the phrase 'all creatures great and small' in the hymn *All Things Bright and Beautiful*. His is a gentle spirituality which comes from a profound wisdom, in which business with soul is ultimately about not succumbing to illusion.

We began our conversation by asking Walter how he came to create Famiglia Mancini. He started by talking about his experiences growing up by the municipal market, where there was both abundance and poverty side by side:

> I come from an Italian family, and I was born by the side of the Mercado Central. I grew up inside of the Mercado Central, which is a magical universe, where there were market stallholders of various origins – Chinese, Japanese, Lebanese, descendants of Spanish, Italians. Normally where you have a lot of food, you have a lot of poverty. When you live in this environment from an early age, with all of these different colours of souls, if you have the sensitivity and perception, all of these things will enter into you and will start to construct who you are. If you could read my body, you could find things from millions of years ago like the remnants of pearls, scales, gills, fins – all evidence of evolution. Maybe this is the original DNA which exists in all creatures. Your DNA carries on and changes; you will change because

of your sensibilities, and these will be polished by the attitudes you see in these other creatures.

Starting to work early in your life at the market, with thousands of people in transit, circulating around there, all of this enters into yourself. You don't notice that all of these things are entering, you don't realise, but one day you finally understand that you are the sum of all of the attitudes which people had around you, all of the sentiments, this is what forms a human being.

You may ask why I came to open a restaurant. I ended up doing this because I had the need to. When you have difficulties in life, it's just like when you are sad, you lean against the person who you are the closest to, for that person will listen to you. Business can be like this. When you have a need and decide to open something, you will have a tendency to create a business which you have the most familiarity with. As I grew up around the market, people mixing with people, I became a merchant. I am not the result of a formal education. I am the fruit of the street, I am the fruit of these creatures. At the end I understood that there is no book more alluring and bewitching than the soul of another. The soul of another is the greatest book. So I learned through life.

While never referencing the great spiritual traditions of India, there are some notable similarities between Walter's philosophy and his innate sense of non-attachment, with the meaning of Maya which is generally translated as 'illusion' or 'unreality':

One of the things I learnt from my mother, when we were living in a humble terraced house, my mother said, "Pay attention to what I will say to you. The only things that will leave with you when you leave this world is the goodness that you did, the goodness that you do for others and forget, and how many times you were able to smile".

Everything that you see here, this furniture, this table, the lights of this restaurant, all of this is an illusion. The only real thing is love and the goodness you do for others. So what happens? When you learn that there is nothing so enticing and fascinating than making other people happy, you forget money. There are people who come into the world to count money, and other people come into the world to love, be loved, learn with the world, and depart. I am this creature. I never chased after money, I always chased my dream. When material things are not the most important things in your life, when material objects are not the structure of your life, when the structure of your life is love, giving, receiving affection and *calor humano*, you will be successful with certainty.

The most meaningful currency in my temple is that you feel happy in my home (restaurant) because it is yours as well. It's not money which drops into the cash register. Why is this? Because money is only money and no more. But emotions, feelings, love, affection, memories, these are the whole universe, everything you have in life. So some friends lent me some money and helped me because before I opened the restaurant I was in a challenging situation, but I ended up opening Famiglia Mancini. That house for me has the fingerprints of God on it. I asked God so much to give me a path for my life, that God finally gave me one.

You are interviewing me, but who I am is just what other people made me. Power doesn't exist, it is an illusion. No one has power in the universe. The only absolute power in the universe is time. This is absolute. Inside time is death, the sacred, and God, because time is eternity and immortality. That which we do not have. Considering this fragility, you have to make a choice.

A long time ago I started to think about time, and nowadays I am not young anymore, I am 74. I was thinking that I entered this world naked and curved. Loving and being loved. When I opened my eyes and I looked at my mother, I loved her and she loved me. I am living my life in order to leave this world in the same form as I came into it, naked, curved, loving and being loved. This is what a real fortune in the world means, the fortune of life, because everything else remains on the earth.

When you discover this dependency, that even when you pass away you need other people because you need someone to carry you to your grave, you need a certain humility in life. I am not the sovereign of my work, sovereign of this whole. The sovereign is that person who chose me. Being chosen in the third largest city in the world to have the restaurant is a privilege.

Walter spoke to us of his sense of being in somehow 'chosen' by a higher consciousness or spirit to create his restaurants. He speaks with humility and an awareness of just how much he has achieved, understanding that not just anyone could have created what he did. One of the key themes of our conversation was generosity, and this is a quality in someone which can only come from love. Nowadays in Brazil it is common for restaurants to offer self-service buffets, in which a person pays for only that which they place on their plates. In the 1980s, Walter was an innovator and was the first person to lay out a range of appetisers ('antipasto') on a table, recreating the abundance and spirit of the Mercadão which he experienced as a child. When explaining this to us, he used the term 'expose' in a poetic manner, a phrase we have kept in translation:

> If you were to ask me how it is possible to be chosen – you can only be loved if you love. You can only receive if you are generous and someone who gives. At the Famiglia Mancini restaurant I decided to recreate what I used to see in the market when I was a child. I was the first person to 'expose the antipasto'. It was like a window display.
>
> This has a seduction because this is generosity. Love from the heart is like a child. It is always a child; it does not register anything, it only feels. The proof that it does not register anything can be seen when you love someone a lot but that person does not love you back, so you promise yourself that you will never love again. But love does not understand this, it always starts from zero. Love has a twin sister – generosity. Every love must be generous otherwise it is not a pure love. It is not real.
>
> When you have exposed all of this food (antipasto), everything which I wanted to happen happened – and when the person, for instance, takes an olive and tastes it, this is liberty, this is generosity, this is what I have to give, this is abundance. This was a revolution in Famiglia Mancini, in 1980. People became happy and grateful with this spontaneity, the idea of choosing exactly what you wanted without other people seeing what you were taking. This is a concrete way in which I could say to my guests that I was happy that you came to my restaurant, look what I did for you.

In 2016, the economic crisis which Brazil had been suffering for some years increased further, with many companies making thousands of employees redundant, and people suffering from a rise in the cost of living, with those with the lowest incomes suffering the most due to significant rises in the prices of basic foods. One item of food which rose more than most was tomatoes, one of the main ingredients in Italian cuisine. While the response of many other restaurants was to reduce the quality of their dishes, the quantity served, or to raise prices, Walter took a different approach:

> When tomatoes went up in price, various restaurants made dishes without tomatoes because they were so expensive. This is disrespect for the client. The client who supported your business for years, the price of tomatoes goes up and you do not use them any more. It is not respectful. The focus is not on the client but on the profit. If I have to pay a little more, I will not keep to the same price, so you won't have them. There is nothing more disrespectful than this. You leave your house, you deal with heavy traffic, you chose this restaurant instead of any of the other 25,000 in São Paulo, you come here and I say to you, 'there is no tomato sauce because tomatoes are expensive'. You will think that I am crazy, and that I don't know what I am doing.

> A restaurant is a type of work where you have to be generous. If you are not generous you can do other things. We grow up with generosity, with our mother putting things on our plate and our father putting things on our plate. The generosity is such that you can serve yourself from the table. But you go to a restaurant and it is not generous. Sometimes some restaurants deal with economic crises by reducing the quantity or reducing the quality. So this is doing the worst thing as they will lose a customer. The most important thing is that you feel happy. It is not a number, it is a relationship. I don't have anything, I am just administering.

Walter's approach to the customer experience, therefore, is that entering any business should be the same experience as being a guest in someone's home. When a guest enters, for example, "they receive a welcoming smile, a glass of water, some wine". The transcendentals in the holonomic circle are drawing our attention to a higher sense of qualities that we normally consider to be subjective or normative, for example 'beauty'. But when we enter into the lived experience of these qualities, as Walter is able to do effortlessly, we see the connection between the transcendentals and how they can manifest concretely within the customer experience, in our experience of generosity and sharing, and in taking a more enlightened approach to our relationship with money:

> The world nowadays is different from the world I grew up in. It is computerised, there are lots of rules, there are studies and marketing research, there are techniques. People ask me if I did market research, but I never did any. I have a rule. I follow a dream and for me the belief of 'will not work out' does not exist. 'This will work out' is what I believe because I am dealing with life, the soul, and I am not looking for money. I am looking to make a dream come true.

> There is something very interesting. You can reach the end of your life full of money, but it continues being only money. What purpose does this money serve at the end of your life? You will buy a frame and put it on a table beside your bed. You can buy slippers, you can travel, you do not have any more deluded desires of having an expensive car, or silk shirts. But this isn't it.

> When you open the archive of your soul, you can see how much you loved and how much you were loved, how happy you made people, there is your fortune and riches. It's not

in the money. It is in the happiness of having given, and sharing. The word 'sharing' – to divide – is like the multiplication of the fishes by Christ. This is beauty. Go, use, eat, be happy. This is beauty.

Since opening in 1980 the Mancini restaurants have received over ten million guests. As a successful entrepreneur, Walter has been interviewed by journalists, appeared on television and has given many lectures to business executives. In relation to the trinity of authenticity at the heart of the holonomic circle, Walter does not change his way of speaking or attempt to conceal his being for a business audience. In doing so he is able to make an impact on business executives and leaders in a manner that few others are able to:

> If you were to ask me 'do you think your story is here (in the restaurant)?', no – I am looking for immortality. I want to see what exists beyond life. Because here I have already seen everything, and now I know. I know what it takes to seduce you and enchant you. Because it's simple. I do not need to be wise. I give my heart to you and I will be happy. This is the essence of history and commerce. I know that I am going against the flow to some extent.

> I know because I have given lectures to senior executives and I have seen executives crying. One of the executives who was crying profusely came to me and I asked him why he was crying. The executive said that it was because I was able to speak about God. "We executives are not able to do this. We are hard and technical. Opening the heart, speaking of God, you talk about needs, you talk about love. An executive can't talk about these things to their staff." They would feel shame to speak about these things.

Life does not function this way. You fragment your heart. So you can talk to your son about God, but you can't talk about God to the person who helps you. This is a terrible mistake because you are not being true. You must be coherent and you must be authentic. I am this. It doesn't matter what other people think about you. I came here and I want the best for you and I want you to help me. This is the curious thing.

The lessons that Walter can teach us extend far beyond those businesses which relate to customer service. While of course there are times when senior executives do require privacy, for example when discussing information which is sensitive to the share price, business leaders do need to be accessible to people across the whole organisation. Business cultures vary dramatically, from those such as Spotify which excel in the practice of dialogue and communication, to those organisations in which status, power and the opinions of the senior executive are prioritised and valued far higher than any contributions from individuals lower down in the organisation. For Walter, this separation and division is one of the worst mistakes that an organisation can make:

There is a mistake which executives make. For example, one executive is promoted. The team helped this person to be promoted. But at some moment that executive will no longer use the same lift as the others any more. You stay, while this person goes up in a special lift.

Walter switches perspective by asking us to imagine that we are now this executive.

I meet you in the hall but I go up in a different lift. This moment marks the start of the most tragic thing which one human does to another human – discrimination. You are now no longer equal anymore. You are in debt to other people because of where you are now but this is something which you have forgotten. One day you will not be in the lift going up any more. You will be in a heliport and no one can see you any more. Even your friends can't speak to you because you are so full of meetings. But at some moment you become old and you look around and ask yourself, 'What do I have? Who stayed with me? And the others who I left behind?' It is like letting go of the hand of one of your children who is then left alone in the world.

On a number of different occasions Walter said to us that he was conscious of going against the flow of what is generally thought of as common business practice and attitudes. But he has a deep-seated sense of his own being, which is rooted in authenticity and a profound sense of love. In chapter three we discussed the four ways of knowing: thinking, feeling, sensing and intuition. It is clear that for Walter, there are some qualities of business leadership which cannot be reduced to just verbal descriptions and measurements; intuition is required for their complete understanding. Love is experienced in the moment, as pure feeling, and, as described by Walter, it does not have a memory which registers the acts and words of others:

And so I am going against the flow based on what I am telling you. I give my heart to the world. What you think about me, and the fact that I have given my heart will not change my way of being, because it will always be this way for a person who loves and who only knows love. The heart forgets and never registers, and it will always be like this. And so Famiglia Mancini was born.

Maybe you can't explain success. In some types of business you can explain success in terms of the production line, technical assistance, they have competitive prices, and you have a competitive advantage and these are one measure of success. This is about success in another language of which I have no knowledge. I would never be hired in a company like this because people would say that this person does not know what he is talking about. He lives a life of delusion, by dreams. But life is like this. Each person is who they are.

Another great lesson for business leaders, especially those who experience great success in their lives, is how to deal with the question of pride. There is very little in the business literature about those qualities necessary for dealing with success. Normally success is defined in terms of financial results, with little attention given to the impact that success has on the character and attitude of an individual. Walter shows that while it is possible not to have a certain type of pride, on the other hand he does have the self-awareness of the personal qualities he has as a leader and entrepreneur in order to have achieved everything that he has done, something which is clearly extraordinary:

One day my wife said to me that I am a strange person because I do not have any pride in what I have built. I think that you will find my reply to her interesting. In my left hand I have a *pires*, a type of saucer which beggars used to use when asking for money. God dances over the top of the *pires*, dancing his light, and so the light of God is dancing on my hand. I am asking God for things, and God provides for me. What I am worth is a plate of lentils and a slice of bread. With this I am feeding people along my way. Is there a moment of having pride in my life? Yes, there is. It is the moment when God comes from heaven and brings to me someone who is in darkness. I have a lantern in my hand, and I put this lantern in the hand of that person, and I say to them that I am putting this lantern in their hand because God asked me to. I say to the person 'Go in this direction, because in this direction you will be happy'.

One day it was raining at night – all the street lights were on. I was leaning against the window looking out. I said to myself that you cannot be proud of everything you have done, but, with a begging bowl in your hand, not just any-one could have built this. This work is not for anyone, but it is possible for someone who knows love, and who loves, who dreams and who has the desire to bring happiness to others.

A visit to one of the Famiglia Mancini restaurants is not just an experience of a single restaurant, it is an experience of wholeness, which starts with the entry into the road Rua Avanhandava. In order to fully grasp this wholeness, we need to achieve a level of consciousness which operates from all four ways of knowing the world. While we previously described Famiglia Mancini in the section 'Identity and Difference' in chapter six, we can now see how the customer experience which Walter has built fully encapsulates Plato's sense of the transcendentals, all of which contribute to a sense of being, and all of which are inseparable interwoven threads of the same cloth. Given that each restaurant has a very clear sense of identity and personality, we asked Walter how he approached the design of each one in a way which still managed to retain this sense of wholeness:

I put things on the walls with a hammer and nails. In the restaurants there are decorative items that I love and that I have made. There are some pictures, for example, which I painted myself. It was I who chose these things, placing them in each restaurant. I can't wear my neighbour's suit to work. I have to wear my own clothes. I can't live in a house whose soul is of the architect or the interior decorator. I have to live inside my own soul. I have to work inside my soul.

Everything which is inside Famiglia Mancini I chose, I put up, and I love. This is what I mean by 'sharing' – I am sharing my intimacy with you. So when you enter the restaurants why is there a unity? It is because it is the same soul which created everything. It comes from the same source of water.

In developing his answer, Walter returned to the themes of generosity and beauty. During our interview we had a copy of *Holonomics* on the table, and in his answer Walter picked it up to develop his metaphor of what is living and what is dead:

This kind of work I did because I am generous in giving. Draws do not serve for anything. They are like graves. Everything you put inside a draw dies. You keep things from other times inside draws for yourself. Some of my friends said I was a crazy person because when I was young and lived alone I used to rip out pictures from beautiful books in order to put them on the wall. If a picture were to stay inside a book it would be dead.

A book could enter a library and stay there. You could say that it is a library, but I could say that it is a cemetery of paper. If you talk about the book to other souls, if you show what is inside it to other people, if I were to read this book, if I were the book, if I live the book in my daily life, I will give life to the book when it goes into my soul. If I pass it on to you, and you pass it on to someone else, and so on and so on, then nothing will die.

If I placed one thing which I like in my house, and then another thing in my house, I would become one of the most tragic things which exists, and that is a collector. He is melancholic, because he takes from another, and confine the world. He confines beauty. Why is a museum beautiful? Because it shares, and everyone can see what is there. Everyone can enjoy it. Is this restaurant my museum? Yes it is, and you can come and see it. Having – the desire to have things – is a grave. It serves no one.

Why are you here? Why did you ask me about the unity? It is because you perceive it. If I kept all of these things in my home you would not be here asking me your questions. To sum up, I offer what I have to people, and say thank you to those who come.

In the previous chapter we looked at how Simon designed an event for Hospital Sírio Libanês which could facilitate a shared sense of meaning among collaborators. This shared sense of meaning came from a dynamic understanding of the relationship between the parts and the whole, the people and the cultural context in which they experienced their work and their relationships with other staff, patients and visitors. Having already spoken of *calor humano*, Walter compared the experience of a hospital to that of a restaurant:

When a patient goes to hospital, he is looking for the materialisation of God in the doctor, because he is very fragile. The only thing he is looking for in hospital is support, affection. Of course this affection starts in the reception. When you come to a restaurant, you come with the spirit of celebration, but in a hospital it is totally different.

To visit a Mancini restaurant is to be temporarily transported to another world, where you enter an Aladdin's cave of curiosities. The experience is not one of a haphazard collection of random items – there is a clear sense of each decorative item belonging together with the others, out of which comes a sense of authentic wholeness. Walter recalled one truly remarkable story which reveals the depth of meaning that these items have, not only for himself but also for those who visit his restaurants:

> Many years ago I was living alone in a tiny bedsit and I had a parrot which was my companion. When I started Famiglia Mancini, I took my parrot to the restaurant because it was my friend throughout the difficult times that I had experienced. When I started the restaurant it marked the start of a period of abundance, and so it was only fair to have my very close friend with me.

> I used to take the parrot to the restaurant, put him inside a cage, and at the end of the evening I used to sit at a table, open the cage, drink some wine, place the parrot on the table. Children who came to the restaurant with their parents used to play with the parrot.

> One day the health inspector said that I could not have an animal in the restaurant, and so I kept the parrot at home. Some years went by. I married and had a son, who accidentally opened the cage. The parrot flew out of the cage and into the neighbour's garden, where it was killed by their dog.

> Many years later I was walking along the street when I had a tap on the shoulder. One man asked me, "And what about the parrot?" I said, "Parrot?" and the guy said, "Yes, the parrot you used to have at the restaurant, 30 years ago. I used to come with my parents and play with him". I told him that

the parrot died and the guy went away. The next day I met the guy again and he said, "Do you remember me?" I answered, "Yes of course, from yesterday". He said to me, "Do you know what I would like you to do? It is for you to have a cage and you can put a parrot made from material inside, because I would like to write my name on a piece of paper and put this paper inside the cage, in order to be forever with the parrot". After saying this he went away. He challenged the wrong man! I bought a gold-coloured cage. I phoned a friend who is an artist and who works with papier-mâché and I told her this story. She said that she would make me a parrot and give it to me as a present. When the parrot arrived, it would not fit in the cage because the door was too small. I phoned another friend who works with metal, and this friend said no problem, he would take the cage apart and put the parrot inside. He made a little place for food for the parrot. This cage is in the same location as where the parrot used to be. The door is open and tied with lace. The cage is there waiting for that man to come and place the piece of paper with his name.

This story makes you understand that I try and build the dreams of others. It is not about money.

Recent years have seen a growing appreciation of the importance of empathy in the design of great customer experiences. However, empathy is not a quality that can be obtained simply through the acquisition of knowledge. We build empathy by developing an ability to enter into the lived experience of other people, an ability which comes when we reach a level of awareness of being in the presence of another human being, another soul. Formal tools such as empathy maps can help us to gain a sense of the experience of others, but there can be no substitution for seeing others from an expanded level of consciousness. This can be seen in the way in which Walter described the change of vibration and the energy in the air at a restaurant as it starts to fill with people:

> A curious thing. Here in the air we can't see it, but there is a serene undulation. When the first client enters, a soul enters, a new vibration. Another comes, then another and another. You can notice that something in the air starts to become vibrant. When the music starts to be played, it triggers a memory inside of you and you start to vibrate differently. When you uncork a bottle and you liberate the spirit of the wine, and modify your emotional state, you create another vibrational state in the air. With a full house, bottles open, music, you can notice that there is a different vibration in the air and the movement of the waiter is different, with a certain electricity. He doesn't walk slowly. He is already rushing. All of these movements? What is this? It is the human being's presence. When you understand that your presence is full of energy and that you can either give a lot of energy or a little for other people, the results are very different. But you must know how to read the results. Entering with a smile is totally different to not smiling.

Walter is alerting us to the fact that we need to understand that the results of our work are as they are due to the energy which we put into it. While this may seem self-evident, there are many organisations and businesses which have such strong cultures that their leaders are not able to perceive clearly the connections between causes and effects. There are many archetypal behaviours and attitudes such as pride, elitism, ego, cognitive dissonance, fear and aggression which can result in extremely faulty diagnoses, such as why people are leaving a company, or why certain managers are not getting the best from the teams which they lead.

The five universal human values of peace, truth, love,

righteousness and non-violence play a central role in the holonomic circle, because when they are present there is sustainability, due to the quality of relationships across the whole. However, nowadays one of the most difficult things to discuss in organisations is loving and sharing. The success of Famiglia Mancini depends on the ability of its leaders, and particularly Walter, to share and transmit his sense of the soul of the restaurants to every single employee. We therefore asked him if he had any particular process or approaches to do this:

> This is something which you do not teach. This is presence of the creature [the leader]. When your conduct and behaviour is decent, clean, earnest and generous and you have ears to hear others, you always have time for listening. When you have the willingness to be open, when you have a good mood, God changes the clock; it is a celestial clock in which the day no longer has twenty four hours, it is infinite. If you have love your clock is infinite; I will work and I will help you.

> When you enter the restaurants and the employees see my demeanour, they can learn very quickly. The person will not learn if you try to indoctrinate them. If you say to them that the organisation wants you to do this and this and this, it does not work because people start to think that you are arrogant. You only accept a master when you are old. When you are young you have difficulties in accepting a master because you are argumentative and question everything. If you sit down and try to teach employees, it seems as if you are a know-it-all, but know-it-alls make people feel uncomfortable. No one has the truth and nothing is static. One situation needs one type of solution, and another situation may require a different solution. So there is no template, or rule or plan to follow.

The middle circle of the holonomic circle is dedicated to tools and techniques. The major insight from this circle is that tools and techniques should not be applied mechanically, without thought to the context, people and present moment. Organisations have elements which are living as well as elements which are fixed, static and non-living, and therefore business processes can also be seen to be in a state of constant change. An example of this is when we encounter waiters who have been given a certain amount of autonomy. When a client encounters a problem, the waiters will seek to solve the problem, but their actions will be moved by the soul of the owners of the restaurant. If the owners are miserly, then the staff will be too.

Customer experiences with soul spring from behaviours and attitudes from people who are moved by the soul of the company. When everyone within an organisation fully understands the purpose, everyone knows what to do and how to act, and so rules and regulations become less necessary, and the company naturally becomes more agile. This idea was expressed beautifully to Walter by his son:

> Some years ago my son said to me, "Dad, you may not be in your restaurants, but whoever goes into the restaurant and knows you knows that your soul is there. They know that it is your home and not that of another, because your spirit is in the house". It is an identity, it is like the use of language of a writer, you read a poem and you know that it comes from that particular writer.

With no formal business training, Walter has managed to find a formula for success which few business ventures of any description have achieved. Perhaps his greatest success is to have solved the great contradiction between money, profit and soul. Coming from a quite humble family background, Walter had to ask for money in order to build his first restaurant, but money does not motivate him. Whereas other people have often struggled with the dilemma of talking about money and soul, Walter has built a business with an exclusive focus is on love, on helping others and to make others happy, which for him is a way of life.

> I am tired of saying this in my lectures, that everyone wants to have a beautiful street. If you love money of any amount you will never renovate and take care of a street. There are two different things. Why is the road so beautiful today? Because while you are walking along the street from one end to the other, you are walking with your dreams. If you deliver to the city one street in which people can be happy, it is wonderful. This is independent of money. A committee of executives from Porto Alegre came to see the street and to hear me speak. In my lecture to them, I said that if you love money you will not manage to have a street like this. Because at the moment when you have to pay the bills for the maintenance of the street, you will have an argument. No one wants to put in money at this moment. I decided to do it alone.

We ended our conversation by asking Walter if he could summarise his philosophy, and if he could articulate the meaning of the soul of Famiglia Mancini:

> The person who thinks they have things is deluded, because no one has anything. We are fragile. We do not know where we are going. Sometimes you can ask yourself if you are a cosmic orphan. Who am I in the universe? Where am I going? I don't have anything. I need love, support, a shoulder to lean on, someone who listens to me. Every person is different from one another. You can't teach this to people. It is difficult.

In all of those places where there is a soul conducting, there is consciousness that you have to live your life in service to others, otherwise it is not worth anything. It makes the soul of love, dedication, care and generosity, always floating in the air inside every place, wherever it is present. My soul has a light of caring, it shines inside all of my restaurants. My profit is your happiness. This is the most beautiful currency I know. Not because of the recognition, but because you know that you are passing through life being useful to others. It is very beautiful that the doors are always open, and each person who comes takes a little of this beauty and this enchantment which is spread amongst the walls, the tables.

When the human being is born and so descends to the world, he or she looks for status, profit, power. This is the great illusion, because you leave with nothing. And if he or she does not love, they leave empty, because they weren't loved. You can't be loved just because you have a superior position in a company. You must be loved because you are beautiful inside. You are loved because you are beautiful, and not because of power. I do not want people to like me because I have the restaurants. I want to be loved because of the soul that I have, because of who I am.

The subtitle for this book is 'A New Era in Design'. The reason for this is that the *Holonomics* approach is based on a foundation of authentic wholeness, a way of knowing the world that requires a new style of learning quite different from that found in the majority of schools and universities today. As Henri Bortoft described it, authentic wholeness means that "the whole is in the part", and so if we are designing an experience, we must pay close attention to the parts instead of general design principles. Business thinking today, either consciously or not, comes from the scientific way of understanding reality, where phenomena are seen as instances of general principles.[155][EN155]

The Famiglia Mancini restaurants are a wonderful environment in which to explore wholeness in this intuitive and phenomenological manner, since it is impossible not to plunge into each decorative item, each one with a story behind it, beautiful in its own right, and yet effortlessly belonging together with every other curiosity, allowing the soul of Walter Mancini to come to presence in our imaginations. In Walter Mancini we find a person for whom there is no differentiation between internal and external. Clients can sense the authenticity each and every time they enter one of his houses as a guest, delighting in the sensory experience, and being touched by his soul, whether he is physically present or not. For this reason in our opening chapter we wrote that "an experience has soul when one soul recognises another soul". Walter Mancini is the absolute epitome of this principle, his entire inner being reflected in the outward creations of his restaurants.

Customer attitudes and sensibilities are changing rapidly, and it is now no longer possible to say that you are one thing when you are not. In a world of ever more transparency, there is no room for pretending to be something and someone – you cannot fake soul. What this means, therefore, is that in order to find authenticity we must urgently start our inner journeys if we have not already done so. This is as true of companies or organisations as it is of individuals. This means moving beyond simply discovering the purpose for our businesses, to discovering how to deliver the purpose and understanding how to put it into practice.

While it is of course possible to connect people emotionally to your purpose, you still have to find a way to put the purpose into practice. The sustainability, resilience and durability of a business can be found in the quality of its relationships, and so it is an illusion to think that financial results can only come from a unilateral focus on financial results. People do not find truth in experiences which are not truly authentic, and these are the types of experiences which cannot endure because inevitably, one day the illusion will become apparent to others. If you really care about creating something that endures, that has roots, there is no way other than authenticity. The truth, therefore, starts with ourselves when there is complete coherence between what we say, what we mean, and how we act.

Great companies are the ones which design customer experiences with soul. A customer experience has soul when it has the quality of authentic wholeness, the principle of life itself. When you can connect with the soul of your organisation and experience the way in which it is expressed through each and every part, you will have created an authentic customer experience with soul.

Endnotes

1   Hans-Georg Gadamer, *Gadamer in Conversation: Reflections and Commentary*, (New Haven: Yale University Press, 2001), p78

2   JUDITE – Estaremos Fazendo o Cancelamento (Fabio Porchat), Anões Em Chamas, https://youtu.be/vEaNCoCXcdk

3   'Customer complaint every second in 2013', The Telegraph, 10th February 2014

4   *For the Good*, Ombudsman Services, 2014/2015 Annual report, accessed from www.ombudsman-services.org/downloads/OS_annualreport_2015.pdf March 2016

5   Matt Watkinson, *The Ten Principles Behind Great Customer Experiences*, (Harlow: Pearson Education Publishing, 2013), Introduction, xv

6   *How to Use Net Promoter to Drive Business Growth*, Deborah Eastman, www.satmetrix.com

7   *2016 Temkin Experience Ratings*, Bruce Temkin, Temkin Group, March 2016, www.temkingroup.com

8   *Ibid.* p5

9   *Employee Engagement Benchmark Study, 2016*, Bruce Temkin, Temkin Group, www.temkingroup.com

10 Jesse Schell, *The Art of Game Design: A Book of Lenses*, (Boca Raton: CRC Press, 2008)

11 *Ibid.* p21

12 *Laces and Hair aposta em produtos orgânicos e cresce 24% no primeiro semestre*, Conta Corrente, Globo News, 21st August 2015

13 Havas' Meaningful Brands® 2015 study, Havas Media, www.meaningful-brands.com. 'Share of Wallet' can be defined as the percentage ("share") of a customer's expenses ("of wallet") for a product that goes to the firm selling the product. Different firms fight over the share they have of a customer's wallet, all trying to get as much as possible. Typically, these

different firms don't sell the same but rather ancillary or complementary product (source: Wikipedia).

14 *Five Human Aspirations and the Future of Brands*, BBMG and GlobeScan, October 2015, www.globescan.com

15 *Histórias contadas pelas marcas Diletto e Do Bem vão parar no Conar*, G1, 25th November 2014

16 *Ibid.*

17 James Watt, *Business for Punks: Break all the Rules – The BrewDog Way*, (United Kingdom: Penguin Random House, 2015), pp.104–105

18 James Watt, *Internal = External*, TEDx Glasgow, 29th June 2016

19 In *Birth of the Chaordic Age*, p24, Dee Hock wrote, "Life is eternal, perpetual becoming, or they nothing. Life is not a thing to be known or controlled. It is a magnificent, mysterious odyssey to be experienced".

20 Johan Wolfgang von Goethe, *Scientific Studies*, (New York: Suhrkamp Publications, 1988), p39

21 Simon Robinson and Maria Moraes Robinson, *Holonomics: Business Where People and Planet Matter*, (Edinburgh: Floris Books, 2014), pp41–43

22 Nigel Hoffmann, *Goethe's Science of Living Form: The Artistic Stages*, (Hillside, NY: Adonis Press, 2007)

23 This figure was originally created by Stephan Harding under the name of The Jungian Mandala (see Stephan Harding, Animate Earth: Science, Intuition and Gaia, 2006, p30). In *Holonomics* we inverted the diagram by placing sensing at the top and intuition at the bottom).

24 Iain McGilchrist, *The Master and his Emissary: The Divided Brain and the Making of the Modern World*, (New Haven: Yale University Press, 2010)

25 Atyeo, Mike and Robinson, Simon (1995) *Delivering Competitive Edge*, Human Computer Interaction: Interact '95, Lillehammer, Norway, pp.384–385

26 Atyeo, Mike, Sidhu, Charanjit, Coyle, Gerry and Robinson, Simon (1996) *Working with Marketing*, Conference Companion on Human Factors in Computing Systems, ACM, New York, Pages 313–314

27 Dan Lyon, *Disrupted: My Misadventure in the Start-Up Bubble*, (New York: Hachette Books, 2016)

28 BrewDog, Annual Report and Accounts for the Year Ending 2016

29 DIY Dog, 25th February 2016, www.brewdog.com/lowdown/blog/diy-dog

30 *Being in the World* directed by Tao Ruspoli, Mangu Films 2014

31 *Ibid.*

32 *Ibid.*

33 Ernst Lehrs, *Man or Matter*, (London: Rudolf Steiner Press, 1951), p19

34 Henri Bortoft, Schumacher College Lecture, 16th September 2011

35 Francis Bacon (1620) *The Great Instauration,* cited in Perez Zagorin, *Francis Bacon*, (Princeton: Princeton University Press, 1999), p251

36 Francis Bacon (1620) Novum organum scientiarum, XXIV, cited in John M. Robertson, *The Philosophical Works of Francis Bacon* (Abingdon: Routledge Revivals, 2011), p329

37 Gabor A. Z. Emplén (2003) The Janus Faces of Goethe: Goethe on the Nature, Aim, and Limit of Scientific Investigation, Polytechnica Ser. Soc. Man. Sci. Vol. 11, No. 1, pp259–278

38 Ernst Lehrs, *Man or Matter*, (London: Rudolf Steiner Press, 1951), p123

39 Henri Bortoft, Schumacher College Lecture, 16th September 2011

40 *Ibid.*

41 Goethe, *Maxims and Reflections*, (London: Penguin Classics, 1999), maxim 279, p34

42 Henri Bortoft, Schumacher College Lecture, 16th September 2011

43 Erazim Kohák, *Idea and Experience: Edmund Husserl's Project of Phenomenology in Ideas I*, (Chicago: University of Chicago Press, 1980), p20

44 Henri Bortoft, Schumacher College Lecture, 16th September 2011

45 ContagiousRadio podcast, April 2015, http://www.contagious.com/ blogs/news-and-views/18100508-interview-with-matt-watkinson -the-now-next-why-podcast-is-here

46 Matt Watkinson, *The Ten Principles Behind Great Customer Experiences*, (Harlow: Pearson Education Publishing, 2013)

47 The worksheets can be downloaded at www.mattwatkinson.co.uk

48 ContagiousRadio podcast, April 2015, http://www.contagious.com/ blogs/news-and-views/18100508-interview-with-matt-watkinson -the-now-next-why-podcast-is-here

49 Fred Reichheld, *The One Number You Need to Grow*, Harvard Business Review, December 2003

50 Net Promoter Network, www.netpromoter.com/know/

51 Rob Markey and Fred Reichheld (2011) *Loyalty Insights: Introducing: The Net Promoter System*, Bain & Company, Inc.

52 *How a New Connected Life Can Transform Communities, and How to Know if Customers Care*, www.sustainablebrands.com, 4th June 2015

53 *Redefining business success in a changing world*, 19th Annual Global CEO Survey, PWC, January 2016

54 *West Lothian Criminal Justice Project*, West Lothian Criminal Justice Project Team, March 2007

55 James Watt, *Business for Punks: Break all the Rules – The BrewDog Way*, (United Kingdom: Penguin Random House, 2015), p75

56 *Ibid.* p76

57 Information in this section retrieved from www.brewdog.com and www.equitypunks.com

58 James Watt, *Business for Punks*, London School of Economics lecture, 19th January 2016

59 *Slam Punk: Equity for Punks IV Ends*, 22nd April 2016, www.brewdog.com/lowdown/press-hub/slam-punk

60 Quotes from John Timpson come from *Hell for Leather*, In Business, Radio 4, Sunday 9th August 2009, reproduced with permission

61 John Timpson, *Upside Down Management; A Common Sense Guide to Better Management*, (Chichester: John Wiley & Sons, 2010)

62 Fritjof Capra and Pier Luigi Luisi, *The Systems View of Life: A Unifying Vision*, (Cambridge: Cambridge University Press, 2014)

63 *Ibid.* p318

64 *Ibid.* p318

65 *Stuck in the middle with Spotify*, The Economist, May 27th 2016

66 Comments are from *Spotify engineering culture (part 1)*, Henrik Kniberg, Spotify Labs, March 27th 2014, labs.spotify.com

67 David Lambert, Chris Chetland, and Craig Millar, *The Intuitive Way of Knowing: A Tribute to Brian Goodwin*, (Edinburgh: Floris Books, 2013), p147

68 Simon Robinson and Maria Moraes Robinson, *Holonomics: Business Where People and Planet Matter*, (Edinburgh: Floris Books, 2014), pp186–188

69 Wells Fargo's phony-account scandal, explained, The Week, September 17th 2016

70 Lakshmi Seetha Ram and K.E. Seetha Ram, *Values Integration for Developing Young Adults*, (San Pedro, Metro Manila: Institute of Sathya

Sai Education, 2004), published under Creative Commons Attribution 3.0 Unported License, viewsandreviewskes.wordpress.com

71 Intel Code of Conduct, www.intel.com/content/www/us/en/policy/policy-code-conduct-corporate-information.html

72 *Ciencia e Tecnologia conversa com Jack Dorsey, criador do Twitter*, May 2013, Globo News

73 Simon Robinson and Maria Moraes Robinson, *Holonomics: Business Where People and Planet Matter*, (Edinburgh: Floris Books, 2014), pp150–153

74 Thomas S. Kuhn, *The Structure of Scientific Revolutions*, (Chicago: The University of Chicago Press, 1962)

75 David Bohm and F. David Peat, *Science, Order and Creativity*, (Abingdon: Routledge Classics, 2011)

76 Simon Robinson and Maria Moraes Robinson, *Holonomics: Business Where People and Planet Matter*, (Edinburgh: Floris Books, 2014), pp82–87

77 For more information about Kyocera's 'Amoeba Management System' see *Holonomics*, pp189–190

78 Hans-Georg Gadamer, *Gadamer in Conversation: Reflections and Commentary*, (New Haven: Yale University Press, 2001), pp89–90

79 Brice Wachterhauser, *Beyond Being: Gadamer's Post-Platonic Hermeneutical Ontology*, (Evanston: Northwestern University Press, 1999), p82

80 *Ibid.* pp81–84

81 Henri Bortoft, *Taking Appearance Seriously: The Dynamic Way of Seeing in Goethe and European Thought*, (Edinburgh: Floris Books, 2012), pp156–160

82 Hans-Georg Gadamer, *Gadamer in Conversation: Reflections and Commentary*, (New Haven: Yale University Press, 2001), p13

83 See for example Hans-Georg Gadamer, *Dialogue and Dialogic: Eight Hermeneutic Studies on Plato*, (New Haven: Yale University Press, 1980)

84 Brice Wachterhauser, *Beyond Being: Gadamer's Post-Platonic Hermeneutical Ontology*, (Evanston: Northwestern University Press, 1999) Weinsheimer, pp187–192

85 *Ibid.* pp67–68

86 Plato, *Statesman*, 311a. This translation comes from Plato, *Complete Works*, edited by John M. Cooper and D.S. Hutchinson, Hackett Publishing Company, 1997

87 Hans-Georg Gadamer, *Truth and Method* (Second Revised Edition, (London: Continuum, 2004), p475

88 Brice Wachterhauser, *Beyond Being: Gadamer's Post-Platonic Hermeneutical Ontology*, (Evanston: Northwestern University Press, 1999), pp122–128

89 Hans-Georg Gadamer, *Gadamer in Conversation: Reflections and Commentary*, (New Haven: Yale University Press, 2001), p75

90 Joel Weinsheimer, *Gadamer's Hermeneutics: A Reading of Truth and Method*, (New Haven: Yale University Press, 1985), p98

91 Hans-Georg Gadamer, *Gadamer in Conversation: Reflections and Commentary*, (New Haven: Yale University Press, 2001), p71

92 *Ibid.* p79

93 Alex Osterwalder and Yves Pigneur, *Business Model Generation*, (Hoboken: Wiley, 2010)

94 Alex Osterwalder, *The Business Model Ontology: A Proposition in Design Science Approach*, Diplômé postgrade en Informatique et Organisation (DPIO) de l'Ecole des HEC de l'Université de Lausanne, 2004

95 *Ibid.* p2

96 The example of Hamlet comes from Henri Bortoft, *Taking Appearance Seriously: The Dynamic Way of Seeing in Goethe and European Thought*, (Edinburgh: Floris Books, 2012), p110

97 For more information on Mangue Bit see for example *Maracatu, Ciranda and Mangue Bit*, World Routes, BBC Radio Four, 7th February 2009 and Daniel B. Sharp, *Between Nostalgia and Apocalypse: Popular Music and the Staging of Brazil*, (Middletown: Wesleyan University Press, 2014)

98 *Caranguejos com cérebro*, pt.wikisource.org

99 Interview with Fernando Peire, Director of The Ivy, London Book Fair, 7th October 2013, www.londonbookfair.co.uk

100 The quotes from Walter Mancini are taken from the videos on their channel *Os segredos da Famiglia Mancini*, youtube.com/user/famigliamancini/videos

101 Henri Bortoft, *The Wholeness of Nature: Goethe's Way of Science*, (Edinburgh: Floris Books, 1996), p16

102 Hans-Georg Gadamer, *Truth and Method* (Second Revised Edition, (London: Continuum, 2004), p121

103 *Ibid.* p121

104 Dr Maria Economo, *Evaluation Strategy for the re-development of the displays and visitor facilities at the Museum and Art Gallery*, Kelvingrove,

June 1999, Humanities Advanced Technology and Information Institute, University of Glasgow

105 Hans-Georg Gadamer, *Truth and Method* (Second Revised Edition, (London: Continuum, 2004), p477

106 *Ibid.* p475

107 Goethe, *Verses in Art,* quoted in Rudolph Steiner, *Nature's Open Secret: Introductions to Goethe's Scientific Writings,* (Herndon: Anthroposophic Press, 2000), p276

108 Steiner, Rudolph, *Colour,* (Forest Row, East Sussex: Rudolph Steiner Press, 1992), p18

109 *Ibid.* p36

110 *Ibid.* p40

111 *Ibid.* p67

112 Idries Shah, *A Perfumed Scorpion,* (London: Octagon Press, 2000), pp24–25

113 Brice Wachterhauser, *Beyond Being: Gadamer's Post-Platonic Hermeneutical Ontology,* (Evanston: Northwestern University Press, 1999), p5

114 *Ibid.* p5

115 *Ibid.* p98

116 Hans-Georg Gadamer, *Truth and Method* (Second Revised Edition, (London: Continuum, 2004), p470

117 Brice Wachterhauser, *Beyond Being: Gadamer's Post-Platonic Hermeneutical Ontology,* (Evanston: Northwestern University Press, 1999), pp97–105

118 The Ladder of Seeing was inspired by Chris Argyris' 'Ladder of Inference' (Chris Argyris, 1990, *Overcoming Organizational Defenses: Facilitating Organizational Learning,* Pearson, pp88–89

119 The Ladder of Seeing was also inspired by the work of David Bohm, particularly *On Dialogue,* (Abingdon: Routledge, 1996)

120 Charles Kahn, *The Art and Thought of Heraclitus,* cited in Brice Wachterhauser, *Beyond Being: Gadamer's Post-Platonic Hermeneutical Ontology,* endnote 12, chapter 3, p207

121 Brice Wachterhauser, *Beyond Being: Gadamer's Post-Platonic Hermeneutical Ontology,* (Evanston: Northwestern University Press, 1999), p109

122 These guidelines are inspired by the work of David Bohm. See for example David Bohm, *On Dialogue,* (Abingdon: Routledge, 1996)

123 Face to Face Interview, BBC, 1959

124 Wachterhauser, Brice, *Hermeneutics and Truth*, (Evanston: Northwestern University Press, 1994), p42

125 Gunther Sonnenfeld, *Smart Ecologies*, www.slideshare.net/goonth/smart-ecologies

126 www.cacadoresdebonsexemplos.com.br

127 www.facebook.com/cacadordebomexemplo

128 'Loja Aumenta em 900% o número de clients após elogio no Facebook', Veja São Paulo, 28th April 2016

129 Plato, Complete Works, edited by John M. Cooper and D.S. Hutchinson, (Hackett Publishing Company, 1997), Phaedrus, 246, c, p524

130 Per Espen Stoknes, *Money and Soul: The Psychology of Money and the Transformation of Capitalism*, (Totnes: Green Books, 2009)

131 Cindy Barnes, Helen Blake and David Pinder, *Creating and Delivering Your Value Proposition: Managing Customer Experience for Profit*, (London: Kogan Page, 2009), p7

132 Jonathan, A. Smith, Paul Flowers and Michael Larkin, *Interpretive Phenomenological Analysis: Theory, Method and Research*, (London: Sage, 2009)

133 Henri Bortoft, *Taking Appearance Seriously: The Dynamic Way of Seeing in Goethe and European Thought*, (Edinburgh: Floris Books, 2012), p166

134 Henri Bortoft, Schumacher College Lecture, September 2009

135 Brice Wachterhauser, *Beyond Being: Gadamer's Post-Platonic Hermeneutical Ontology*, (Evanston: Northwestern University Press, 1999), p169

136 *Ibid.* p136

137 *Ibid.* p187

138 See for example Henri Bortoft, *Taking Appearance Seriously: The Dynamic Way of Seeing in Goethe and European Thought*, (Edinburgh: Floris Books, 2012), p26

139 *Ibid.* pp.90–127

140 *Ibid.* p100

141 See *ibid.* pp90–127

142 See for example Mark Wrathall's opening comments, *Being in the World*, Tao Ruspoli, Mangu Films 2014

143 Hans-Georg Gadamer, *Gadamer in Conversation: Reflections and Commentary*, (New Haven: Yale University Press, 2001), p111

144 Mark Wrathal, *Being in the World* directed by Tao Ruspoli, Mangu Films 2014

145 See the section The History of Being, *ibid.*

146 For an extensive treatment of this theme see also the section New Orders in Society in David Bohm and F. David Peat, *Science, Order, and Creativity*, pp98–105

147 *Making the Modern World,* British Science Museum

148 *Ibid.* Curation notes

149 *Being in the World* directed by Tao Ruspoli, Mangu Films 2014

150 Mark Wrathall, *Ibid.*

151 Manuel Molina, *Ibid.*

152 Hubert Dreyfus, *Ibid.*

153 Audrey Yoshiko Seo, *Ensō: Zen Circles of Enlightenment,* (Boston: Weatherhill, 2007), p1

154 *São Paulo's Mercadão – Municipal Market & Meeting Place,* Street Smart Brazil, 16th September, 2015

155 Bortoft, Henri, *Counterfeit and authentic wholes: Finding a means for dwelling in nature,* in Seamon, D and Mugerauer, R (eds.), *Dwelling, Place, Environment: Towards a Phenomenology of Person and World,* Martinus Nijhoff Publishers, Dordrecht, 1985

Bibliography

Argyris, Chris (1990), *Overcoming Organizational Defenses: Facilitating Organizational Learning*, Pearson, Hoboken

Atyeo, Mike and Robinson, Simon (1995) Delivering Competitive Edge, *Human Computer Interaction: Interact '95*, Lillehammer, Norway

–, Sidhu, Charanjit, Coyle, Gerry and Robinson, Simon (1996) Working with Marketing, *Conference Companion on Human Factors in Computing Systems*, ACM, New York

Barnes, Cindy, Blake, Helen and Pinder, David (2009) *Creating and Delivering Your Value Proposition: Managing Customer Experience for Profit*, Kogan Page, London

Bortoft, Henri (1996) *The Wholeness of Nature: Goethe's Way of Science*, Floris Books, Edinburgh

–, (2012) *Taking Appearance Seriously: The Dynamic Way of Seeing in Goethe and European Thought*, Floris Books

Bohm, David (1996), *On Dialogue*, Routledge, Abingdon

–, and Peat, F. David (2011) *Science, Order and Creativity*, Routledge, Abingdon

Capra, Fritjof and Luigi Luisi, Pier (2014) *The Systems View of Life: A Unifying Vision*, Cambridge University Press, Cambridge

Gadamer, Hans-Georg (1980) *Dialogue and Dialogic: Eight Hermeneutic Studies on Plato*, Yale University Press, New Haven

–, (2001) *Gadamer in Conversation: Reflections and Commentary*, Yale University Press, New Haven

–, (2004) *Truth and Method* (Second Revised Edition, Translation revised by Joel Weinsheimer and Donald G. Marshall), Continuum, London

–, (2008) *Philosophical Hermeneutics* (2nd Revised edition), University of California Press, Berkeley

Goethe, Johann Wolfgang von (1999) *Maxims and Reflections*, Penguin Classics, London

Heidegger, Martin (2010) *Being and Time* (translated by Joan Stambaugh) SUNY Press, Albany

Hock, Dee (1999) *Birth of the Chaordic Age*, Berrett-Koehler Publications, San Francisco

Hoffmann, Nigel (2007) *Goethe's Science of Living Form: The Artistic Stages*, Adonis Press, Hillside, NY

Kohák, Erazim (1980) *Idea and Experience: Edmund Husserl's Project of Phenomenology in Ideas I*, University of Chicago Press, Chicago

Kolster, Thomas (2012) *Goodvertising: Creative Adverting that Cares*, Thames & Hudson, London

Kuhn, Thomas S. (1962) *The Structure of Scientific Revolutions*, The University of Chicago Press, Chicago

Lambert, David, Chetland, Chris and Millar, Craig (eds.) (2013) *The Intuitive Way of Knowing: A Tribute to Brian Goodwin*, Floris Books, Edinburgh

Lehrs, Ernst (1951) *Man or Matter*, Rudolf Steiner Press, London

Lyon, Dan (2016) *Disrupted: My Misadventure in the Start-Up Bubble*, Hachette Books, New York

McFadden, David (2005) *Legend of the Rainbow Warriors*, Harlem Writers Guild Press, New York

McGilchrist, Iain (2010) *The Master and his Emissary: The Divided Brain and the Making of the Modern World*, Yale University Press, New Haven

Osterwalder, Alex and Pigneur, Yves (2010) *Business Model Generation*, Wiley, Hoboken

Robertson, John M. (2011) *The Philosophical Works of Francis Bacon*, Routledge Revivals, Abingdon

Robinson, Simon and Moraes Robinson, Maria (2014) *Holonomics: Business Where People and Planet Matter*, Floris Books, Edinburgh

Schell, Jesse (2008) *The Art of Game Design: A Book of Lenses*, CRC Press, Boca Raton

Seamon, D and Mugerauer, R (eds.) (1985) *Dwelling, Place, Environment: Towards a Phenomenology of Person and World*, Martinus Nijhoff Publishers, Dordrecht

Seetha Ram, Lakshmi, and K.E. Seetha Ram (2004) *Values Integration for Developing Young Adults,* Institute of Sathya Sai Education San Pedro, Metro Manila

Seo, Audrey Yoshiko (2007) *Ensō: Zen Circles of Enlightenment,* Weatherhill, Boston

Shah, Idries (2000) *A Perfumed Scorpion,* Octagon Press, London

Sharp, Daniel B. (2014) *Between Nostalgia and Apocalypse: Popular Music and the Staging of Brazil,* Wesleyan University Press, Middletown

Smith, Jonathan, A., Flowers, Paul and Larkin, Michael (2009) *Interpretive Phenomenological Analysis: Theory, Method and Research,* Sage, London

Srur, Eduardo (2012) *Manual de Intervenção Urbana,* Bei Comunicação, São Paulo

Steiner, Rudolph (1992) *Colour,* Rudolph Steiner Press, Forest Row, East Sussex

–, (2000) *Nature's Open Secret: Introductions to Goethe's Scientific Writings,* Anthroposophic Press, Herndon

Stoknes, Per Espen (2009) *Money and Soul: The Psychology of Money and the Transformation of Capitalism,* Green Books, Totnes

Tapscott, Don (2010) *Smart Swarm: Using Animal Behaviour to Change our World,* Harper Collins, London

Timpson, John (2010) *Upside Down Management; A Common Sense Guide to Better Management,* John Wiley & Sons, Chichester

Watt, James (2015) *Business for Punks: Break all the Rules – The BrewDog Way,* Penguin Random House

Wachterhauser, Brice (ed.) (1994) *Hermeneutics and Truth,* Northwestern University Press, Evanston

–, (1999) *Beyond Being: Gadamer's Post-Platonic Hermeneutical Ontology,* Northwestern University Press, Evanston

Watkinson, Matt (2013) *The Ten Principles Behind Great Customer Experiences,* Pearson Education Publishing, Harlow

Weinsheimer, Joel (1985) *Gadamer's Hermeneutics: A Reading of Truth and Method,* Yale University Press, New Haven

Zagorin, Perez (1999) *Francis Bacon,* Princeton University Press, Princeton

Index

About the Authors

Simon Robinson is the co-founder of Holonomics Education, a consultancy which empowers businesses and organisations through a different way of thinking, by helping them to see and understand whole systems. This allows them to implement great customer experiences, powerful and effective strategies, and develop purposeful, meaningful and sustainable brands.

Simon began his career at BT Laboratories (British Telecom) in ergonomics and human factors, responsible for the design of user interfaces and the customer experience of fixed and mobile consumer products. In 1995 with a number of colleagues he developed an approach 'designing the customer experience' which brought together Marketing and Human Factors with more radical perspectives such as semiotics and anthropology, creative and visualisation skills, generating a new approach to user-centred innovation. He is the co-author of *Holonomics: Business Where People and Planet Matter*, a Harvard Business Review author and editor of the blog www.transitionconsciousness.org.

Maria Moraes Robinson is the co-founder of Holonomics Education and an internationally recognised educator and keynote speaker in strategy, change management, customer experience, human values and the Balanced Scorecard methodology. As a leading business strategist Maria worked personally with Robert Kaplan and David Norton introducing and developing the Balanced Scorecard methodology in Brazil and Latin America across many sectors and industries.

Maria is a published author in Harvard Business Review and

is the co-author of the books *Holonomics: Business Where People and Planet Matter, Strategy Management: Experiences and Lessons of Brazilian Companies* and *The Strategic Activist.*

For further information please see www.holonomics.co.uk.

Printed in Great Britain
by Amazon